West of Castle Rock

View from Cartway Cove down the coast to Varley Head with the Port Isaac Terrace in the background

West of Castle Rock

Port Isaac,
For Letter or for Verse
1944–1950

James Platt

All rights reserved; no part of this publication may be reproduced or transmitted by any means, electronic, mechanical, photocopying or otherwise, without the prior permission of the publisher.

First published in Great Britain in 2011 by Creighton Books
Website: www.creightonbooks.nl
Email: jim.platt@planet.nl

© 2011 James Platt

ISBN 978 90 807808 6 6

The moral right of James Platt to be identified as the author of this work has been asserted by him in accordance with the Copyright, Designs and Patents Act 1988

British Library Cataloguing in Publication Data
A catalogue record for this book is available from the British Library

Designed in the UK by
Special Edition Pre-Press Services

Printed and bound in Great Britain by
Lightning Sources UK Ltd

This book is dedicated to the eternal
memory of my dearly beloved wife Maria,
who made of every day a blessing

Maria Filomena Platt-Cornoldi
1 January 1941 – 8 July 2008
Rest in Peace

Painted by René Boelen, 2010

Along the bright path of her life full led,
Clear amber-cherished memories gently flow,
Her tapestry was wrought from loving thread,
Her joyfulness of spirit made it glow.

So fine her touch, and thus her caring good
Set ripples fine to spreading, coalescing,
Warming the hearts of all with her stood -
To know her was to count a lifetime blessing.

Her spirit guides the steps of those she loved.
They guard the light of her eternal ember
In hope, integrity and greatness proved.
She is not gone, as long as we remember.

Also by James Platt and published by Creighton Books

East of Varley Head—Stories from Port Isaac, North Cornwall
1945–1950

Published in 2003, ISBN 978 90 807808 1 2

Your Reserves or Mine?

Published in 2004, ISBN 978 90 807808 2 0

South of Lobber Point—More stories from Port Isaac, North Cornwall
1945–1950

Published in 2005, ISBN 978 90 807808 3 9

The Great Tanganyika Diamond Hunt

Published in 2007, ISBN 978 90 807808 4 2

North of Little Hill—Proper Talk in Port Isaac, North Cornwall
1944–1950

Published in 2009, ISBN 978 90 807808 5 9

If, in these modest rhymes and quatrains terse,
The good and lesser good lie tight entwined
In Isaac's Port, for better or for verse—
Then reader seek, and mayhap ye shall find.

And if the metre falters on the letter,
Read on! Perhaps the next verse will scan better.

There is a repose about Lant Street, in the Borough, which sheds a gentle melancholy on the soul. There are always a good many houses to let in the street: it is a bye-street too, and its dullness is soothing. A house in Lant Street would not come within the denomination of a first-rate residence in the strict acceptation of the term; but it is a most desirable spot nevertheless. If a man wished to abstract himself from the world—to remove himself from within the reach of temptation—to place himself beyond the possibility of any inducement to look out of the window—he should by all means go to Lant Street. The population is migratory, usually disappearing on the verge of quarter-day, and generally by night. His Majesty's revenues are seldom collected in this happy valley; the rents are dubious; and the water communication is frequently cut off.

Charles Dickens
The Pickwick Papers—chapter xxxii

Contents

	List of Illustrations	*Page* x
	Map of Port Isaac District	xi
	Map of Port Isaac Village	xii
	Foreword—For all the Arts	xiii
1	Les Indigènes	1
2	West of Castle Rock	4
3	On Gaverne Beach	51
4	The Terrace	53
5	Transport at its Best	56
6	At the Pictures	57
7	The Church Rooms	60
8	Hillson's Dump	64
9	The Breakwaters	69
10	Pawlyn's Cellars	71
11	Trewetha Lane	73
12	The Chairs in St Peter's Church	78
13	Games in the School Playground	82

14	A Flea Hunt	*Page* 84
15	Doctor	86
16	The Policeman	89
17	Fight!	90
18	Living in Council Houses	94
19	Church Hill	99
20	St Illick's Well	102
21	On Little Hill	105
22	The Old Mines	106
23	A shilling on the ground	108
24	The Temperance Hall	110
25	The Local Preacher	114
26	The Town Platt	119
27	The Post Office	120
28	Sherratt's Bread	122
29	First Line of Defence	126
30	The Freak Valley	130
31	St Endellion	134
32	Gaggy	136
33	A Callybash	139
34	The Rolls Canardly	140
35	The Cobbler	142
36	The Mill Pool	144
37	The Lake Flush	148
38	Family Favourites	150
39	Varley Sands	154
40	Writing Poetry for the Parish Magazine	155
41	Port Quin	158

42	The Singing Butchers	*Page* 160
43	Skittery Grass (By Maria Platt-Cornoldi)	161
44	The Long Pool	164
45	The Bark House	168
46	Gull's Eggs	170
47	My Friend Ted	173
48	The Likes of They	174
49	Temple Bar	178
50	Scrumpers	180
51	Rose Hill	181
52	Community Values	184
53	Remember the Sabbath Day	188
54	Happy Times	194
55	Journey's End	197
Afterword		198

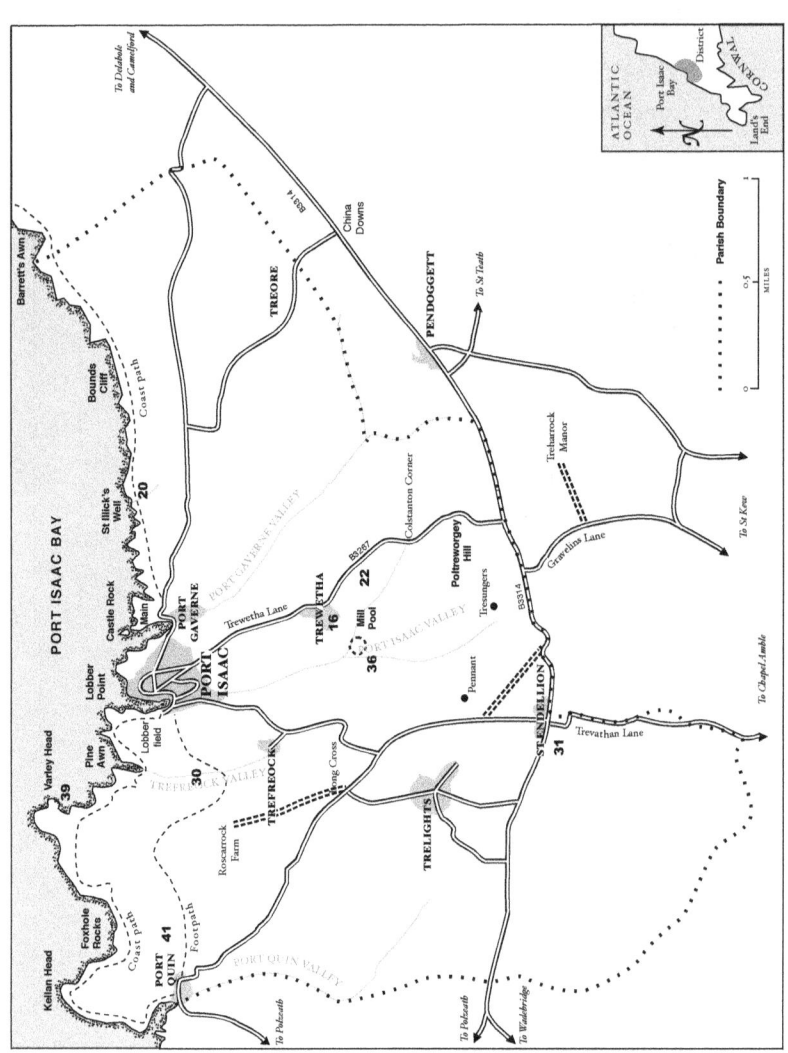

Sketch map of Port Isaac district
(location numbers refer to correspondingly numbered poems)

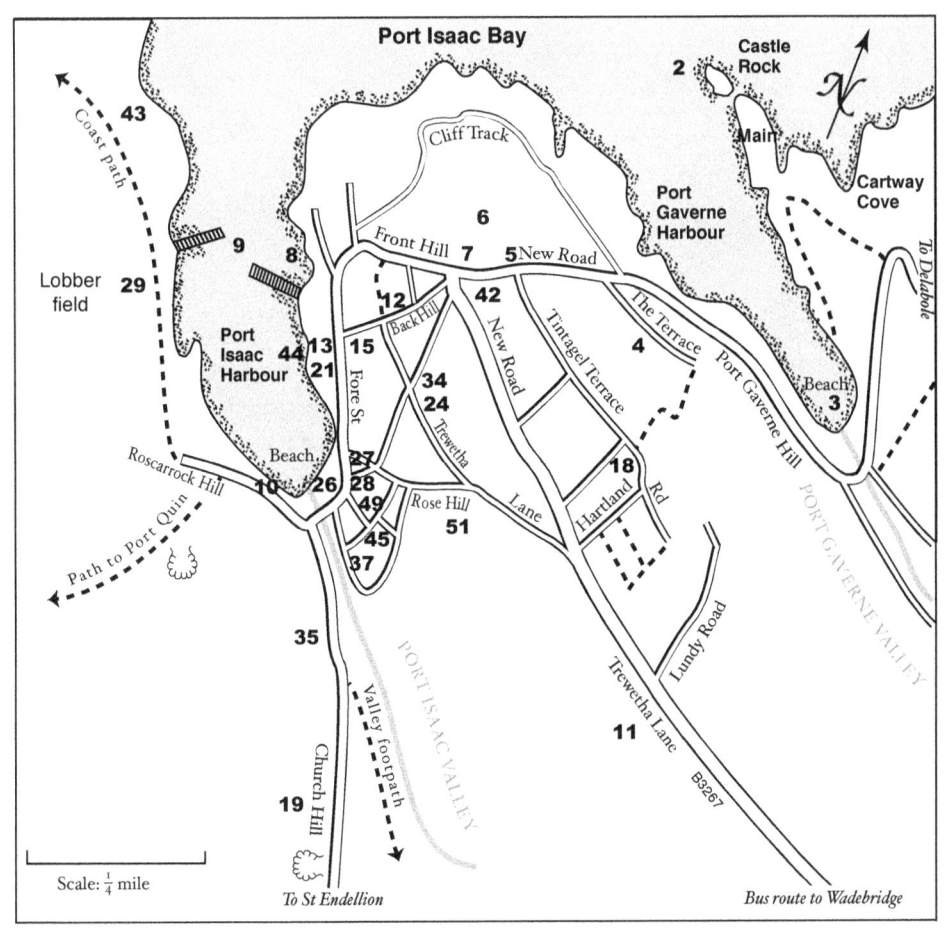

Sketch map of Port Isaac village
(location numbers refer to correspondingly numbered poems)

Acknowledgements

This book was designed and prepared by Corinne Orde and Romilly Hambling of Special Edition Pre-Press Services (www.specialedition.co.uk). The kindness, style, expertise, insight and patience that they brought to the work were impeccable. Corinne's deep care of editing was of fundamental benefit to the qualities of the finished volume.

The book was digitally set and registered for print-on-demand orders with key trade and Internet booksellers and distributors by Lightning Source UK Limited of Milton Keynes (www.lightningsource.com). LSUK's consistent commitment to Creighton Books, together with the company's professional excellence and personal attention was exemplary.

This title assigned to this collection of verses and by extension to the realisation of the verses as a collection was due in no small measure to the encouragement of my great friend and die-hard Spurs supporter Mr Terry Graystone. It was Terry who, on pointing out that as the titles of my three previous books written on a Port Isaac late-1940s theme had each incorporated a cardinal point of the compass, there would have to be a fourth title to close the sequence in an orderly way. Thanks to Terry, *West of Castle Rock* was conceived.

The inspiration for the principal piece of verse in this collection (certainly in terms of its length) and from which the collection takes its title, was the autobiographical "Summoned by Bells" by John Betjeman, himself no stranger to St Endellion parish.

Finally I would like to thank my beloved wife Maria whose guiding hand is always with me.

"And all that's best of dark and bright, meets in her aspect and her eyes".

Foreword

For all the Arts

In the decade immediately following the end of the Second World War, we who formed the community of the village of Port Isaac in North Cornwall still revelled in an isolation which we held onto as much by choice as by necessity. We thrived on the undoubted fact of our shared quality of unique superiority in comparison to any other village community in the county, and this understanding rang for us like a fine bell with its own casting of pride.

There was a great tradition of song amongst us, and although soloists of ability slotting in anywhere between alto-soprano and basso-profundo were admittedly in short supply, a variety of established choirs provided a clear demonstration of there being safety in numbers.

A close-harmony quartet, with the original name of "The Four in Harmony" was celebrated not only in Port Isaac itself but far into the wild country beyond the village borders. Their rendition of "Silver Threads Among the Gold" was guaranteed to bring an audience to tears.

The essential fount of choral endeavour sprang out of the two local chapel congregations. The church also made a contribution, but was unable to compete to any advantage with the talent for singing that chapel people had. It was well known that the latter's repertoire included much better and far more rousing songs than did the church song book. For chapel people, lusty-voiced choral activity provided an alter-ego counterpoint to the advanced degree of petty-mindedness that was their least endearing characteristic.

There was, in addition, a manifestation of choral singing at the primary school. It may not have been done well, but it was done with passion, and that was more than enough to provide every grimy-kneed vocalist with satisfaction. Perhaps most notably in the school context, church and chapel voices were often raised in song together and without rancour—or at least with rather less rancour than was practised across the great religious divide by most of the school pupils' elders and betters.

Original pantomimes and Christmas concerts, written by a group of village residents (among whom school teachers were in the ascendancy) were performed by local casts (recruited both with and without coercion) on the stage in the Temperance Hall up in lower Trewetha Lane. The productions were sparklingly popular highlights of early winter after the evenings had drawn in, and when, apart from huddling in the midst of a crowd in the Temperance Hall, the only other place to keep warm was to be at home sitting much too close to the fire.

The board-treading scene in Port Isaac was further graced by fairly regular contests presenting a variety of home-grown talent, the word "talent" being used under advice. Such contests took place on the stages of both the Temperance Hall and the Church Rooms located up at the top of Front Hill. In the summer months, when a mighty host of visitors came to stay in hotels up on the Terrace, here and there in the rest of the village and down in Port Gaverne, some of these foreigners could easily be persuaded to lend their own talent to a show, and be not averse to accepting the momentary fame that ensued and/or alternatively taking abject humiliation in their stride.

A Port Isaac audience knew what it liked. Unfamiliar material, not least if it was of a *risqué* variety, sometimes promoted vociferous unease in the seats at the back of the auditorium.

The height of achievement in our local culture of performing arts was almost certainly scaled by the Port Isaac Drama Group, a repertory-styled company with quasi-professional pretensions which staged a summer season each year with a once-weekly performance of a play in the Temperance Hall. Since the schedule of visitors involved a more or less complete changeover every fortnight, the plays put on by the Drama Group could always count on a replenishment of fresh clientele in its audiences. Hence they invariably played to full houses. The plays were either murder mysteries or light drawing-room comedies. They were intended to entertain. Unhappy endings were not appreciated in Port Isaac.

In the Temperance Hall and Church Rooms, Port Isaac could then boast of having two legitimate theatres available to benefit its community. That was not bad for a village of only about a thousand souls. If Charlie Lobb's converted garage, more formally known as the Rivoli Cinema (screenings every Friday evening) was taken into account, that went on to make not just two but three village theatres to be marvelled at as cultural assets.

On an individual level, both in and out of the home, village craftwork was very much alive, conducted for pleasure, or to kill time, or to fulfil a pressing need. Needlework and embroidery of a splendid quality were commonly practised household skills, passed on down through generations.

Weaving and splicing of ropes and cordage, and the associated neat tying of intricate knots and designs, were part and parcel of the local fishermen's core base of artistry.

Some fishermen were also experts in whittling, and many more in durable basket making, as exemplified in the large two-man carrier baskets known as mawns, and by a seemingly endless production line of crab pots, each of which was an individual work of art in its own right. The pots were woven from pliant withies cut from carefully husbanded willow trunks growing in the Mill Pool up in the heart of the Port Isaac valley.

Commendable though the arts and crafts output may have been in the aesthetic sense, none of it fell into the category of representing art for art's sake. The underlying motivation and purpose for making any item was always directed towards a practical endpoint. The inherent beauty of each product resulted from generations of experience in creating the best that was possible in order to match the function for which it was intended. Necessity set the rules, but the spirits of a succession of craftsmen contrived to ensure that embellishments were always called on to please the eye of the beholder.

The understanding, the care, and the meticulous management of materials wrought by so many practised hands let a golden touch of poetic appreciation flow subliminally into so many aspects of life in Port Isaac. Yet had we known that this was how it was (and generally we didn't), not a man-jack among us would have admitted to knowing it.

When the visitors were around, a normal sight at various recognised advantageous locations in the village was an artist seated behind a small easel bearing a frame-stretched rectangle of canvas on which the artist would be attempting to paint an impression of the view that he or she was beholding. It was possible to encounter as many as half a dozen such painters scattered around the place on any given day of clement weather. Passers-by tended to halt in the commission of their passing by not passing by at all. They gathered in quite substantial groups behind the work in progress in order to comment at length, not always favourably, on the artist's technique and within the artist's hearing.

It was street entertainment of a high order. Some artists were better than others, but the bar was not always set too high. Time, which was available in abundance, was squandered in full measure at the rear of the artist's shoulders. The artist had no alternative but to grin and bear it.

As onlookers who would have been affronted if we had heard ourselves being described as kibitzers, we were not especially interested in the burgeoning victory, impending disaster or perhaps unsatisfactory truce slowly manifesting itself on the canvas. Our focus was not aimed at the What as it was at the Why.

Why paint that? Why would someone want to paint a picture of the harbour, a few fishing boats at their moorings, the Town Platt, Lobber Cliff, or a few whitewashed cottages lining the side of a narrow lane? If anyone among us wanted to see what those things looked like, all we had to do was open our eyes and gawp—and not for too long as well. After all, to us there was nothing extraordinary about a local view.

If the fancy ever took us to look at a picture of a view, we could go and buy a postcard down in Mrs Rowe's newspaper shop on the lower bend of Fore Street, or even up in the top part of Mrs Cowling's chemist's shop at the bottom of Back Hill, just across the road from the school. Admittedly the postcards were a bit grainy in texture, but that was always the case with sepia tints and black and white, and the Frith representations of views were perfectly adequate as subjects to engage our eyes.

What there was to see all around us was simply there, and it would be there tomorrow, just as it would be in a year, a decade or a century from now for the predilections of the few among us who were motivated to look that far ahead.

We knew as well that there was always likely to be a problem in what any one of us might do with one of the completed paintings if it was acquired. Hanging it up on the cottage wall was only going to result in the eventual appearance of a remnant of its shape outlined in dark grey when the string broke, or the nail fell out and the picture came down.

For all of what must have been many thousands of painted canvases and untold hours of artistic effort that went into capturing images of Port Isaac in oils, or watercolours or acrylics, or (if you were Ted Robinson) in gouache, the vast majority of paintings were barely considered by most of us both in their own place and in their own time.

It wasn't as if we Port Isaac folk were all Philistines when confronted by the face and shadow of the arts, although undoubtedly most of us were. It took a certain amount of courage to accept that visual arts were not for the likes of us.

A feeling for the natural beauty of the village, the coast of Port Isaac Bay and the parish hinterland which visitors found so appealing tended to pass us by. We lived with it all every day and took it so much for granted that it seemed altogether mundane. Revelling in its lyric qualities, and reacting to it by expressing and recording emotions and introspective joy was in many ways anathema to our way of thinking, even though our sense of being at one with the area in which we lived was so perfectly formed.

A similar consideration applied to our encounters with and treatment of the written word. For a village and community with a long, rich and vibrant tradition, replete with characters fit to grace the pages of any volume of history, biography, verse, fact thinly disguised as fiction and so on and so forth, there emerged, in the sad light of hindsight, a regrettable lack of documentation.

When I was growing up in Port Isaac I knew of no-one who truly believed that he or she had led a life of any interest at all to his or herself, let alone of interest to third parties. For all of us, what lay in the past was over and done with, was no longer of concern and could be of no conceivable value to anyone else. Besides, not one of us could ever rest easy in the knowledge that a foreigner might be sitting and reading about our personal business on a chair somewhere up the line.

The truth of it was, probably anyway, that too many secrets lurked behind the closed (if rarely locked) doors of Port Isaac. There was too broad a plethora of inter-family feuds held active in spite of their root causes being long lost in the mist of generations past. Most of us held our cards painfully close to our chests. Neighbours existed to be helped in times of trouble, but they were not exactly to be trusted, and along the way it never hurt anyone to take a little pleasure in the misfortune of others.

If things should ever be written down with reference to Port Isaac people, our history and our way of life, it would mean that anyone able to read could come along and read it, and not only that, anyone to whom the written word was a mystery unlikely to be solved could have it read to him. That sort of thing was clearly not to be countenanced.

We knew without question that the history of ordinary people like us was all too often written by people who had had no serious acquaintance with the key influences that shaped our lives.

But then again, if a local personage was to be hauled into court and have the tale of his (very rarely her) misdeeds reported in the pages of the weekly *Cornish Guardian* newspaper, there was obviously a high degree of satisfaction to be taken in running the eye over such gems of topical reading matter.

Port Isaac it was, for letter or for verse.

There was indeed, a lot to sing about.

Downtown Port Isaac centred on the Harbour Beach and the Town Platt

1

Les Indigènes

Port Isaac born! If such you be,
Then fearlessly rejoice!
A heaven appointed destiny!
In gladness raise your voice!

Infuse your soul with fulsome pride,
Enduring, circumspect.
Through life's fair ways the Port will guide
Your steps, steadfast, direct.

When shadows dark impose on days
Weighed down by anxious care,
Then let the rolling ocean's ways
To soothing peace you bear.

If God there be to bless this place,
Its people gently lead,
To live their lives in His good grace,
Fulfilling every need.

They are the folk whose spirits true
The very stones invest.
Ensuring generations new
The solace of the blest.

These lilies of the village street
Toil not, yet do they spin
In rich abandon when they meet,
And loose the ire within.

They rest in St Endellion's clay
Slate shards from sexton's blade.
Scant comfort knew they in their day,
Now know they sacred shade.

Endurance wrote their testament,
Their fulfilment denied,
By circumstance and chance full spent,
Lost hope and foundered pride.

Their worth lay not in copper coin
Or ever-jealous gold.
But who they were did gird the loin
And gilded those the bold.

Their cherished lives to most unmarked
In solitude displayed.
As priceless gems which blazed and sparked
Through countless years arrayed.

Theirs was not to bemoan their lot,
Touched forelocks did they own.
They offered deference to what
Were knaves in blue blood sown.

They made the village what it was,
And is and e'er shall be,
They won the land, they conquered loss,
Fought unforgiving sea.

They fished, they dug, they cursed, they spat,
They laughed, they loved, they schemed
With mettle in the Port and Platt —
The morrow scorned, they dreamed ...

Of how the Flush did scour the Lake,
Of mackerel in the pan,
Gulls' eggs for tea and saffron cake,
Two-thirty's also-ran.

O these were men! Their Guernsey'd mien
Held character sublime,
True legends of what might have been,
But for the clutch of time.

With wistfulness let us recall
Their honoured roll of names.
They stand as hallows, One and All,
Belov'd eternal flames.

Port Isaac born! For such were they,
Sweet essence of the tide.
Their spirits soar to greet each day,
Proclaiming local pride.

2

West of Castle Rock

A buzzard drifts on high o'er Gaverne's woods.
Tight spiralled, effortless on fingered wings.
Below, the bluebells flood 'neath greening oaks
And moss-banked stream clinks downwards from Treore.

Circling anew, the buzzard's compass draws
Pendoggett, Delabole, Tintagel's thrust,
To where the Bay sweeps boldly to the Rumps,
Beyond Port Quin and dome-cast Kellan Head.

And pivotal to this most glorious scene,
Port Isaac nests within its cliff-girt Awn.
A thousand souls do call Port Isaac home,
A piscatory place of deep bred pride.

Port Gaverne to the east in somnolence
("Gay-verne" not "Gavverne" do the locals say),
Port Isaac's portal is—first in, then out
Paved full throughout with gifted timelessness.

The road descent slips strait from China Downs,
On Weathered Hill twixt blackthorn tangled walls.
Port Gaverne first, Port Isaac o'er the hill.

A dark road, slated verge above Cartway—
It curves both sharp and deep at rear of Main,
Where rich valerian bursts, pink, scarlet, white
Cascades to beautify the shingled beach
First sighted by the bend below Headlands.

From crumbling, fine-grassed ledge atop the void
The abyss drops to wildly rocky cove
Down crackling bluffs and slippery plated scree.
Familiar of the Bay in all its moods.

High on the cliff's precipitate redoubts
Do fulmars gawp and cackle where they sit.
They waddle crude then launch into the wind,
And saving grace doth take them in its hand.
For these are masters of the restless air.
They ride the eddies with an angel's touch.

Tintagel Head, far limit of the Bay
Into Atlantic plants its blunted face
And surf foams white by feet of greying cliffs,
To stir the mind with thoughts of Camelot.

Hull down on the horizon rides a ship
And there, translucent in the telling eye
Mutely suggested, Lundy Island shows
Whenever curtained squalls do ease their march
And lighthouse pulses pierce the gale-torn night.

O Bay! A sweeping crenulated arc
Few harbours bite into this rocky drift
Of sea-pinked heights and dripping scurvy grass,
And springy turf where myriad rabbits run,
To offer solace to the mariners
Who daily brave its rage, and ply its waves.

Its cliffs are rife with guillemots and gulls
Full raucous in their territorial zeal.

And there are cormorants and razorbills,
And shags bedeck sheer slate declivities.
Three ports defend the fisher's right to live,
Quin, Gaverne, Isaac are their hallowed names,
And of these three Port Isaac bears the crown.

Yet Gaverne calls us from its gullied heights,
Where Headlands hospitality, white-faced,
Besieged by terraced lawn and wind-racked shrubs
(Non-residents all welcome so they say),
Commands attention from itinerants.

Look stranger, look o'er Gaverne's mottled strand,
And bubbling stream that from Pendoggett comes,
To cob-walled cellars in which sparrows nest
And venerable slates stand firm on roofs.

Across the valley cast the wand'ring eye,
O'er beach side wall, crisp gorse and brambled drift,
And flowing blackthorn, mirror of the wind.
For there walled bulwarks of Port Isaac stand,
Exposed to slash of rain and booming gales.

Implacable as sculptured monoliths
See council houses loom stark and supreme.
Rough cast are both the sides and residents,
Gull-spotted roofs with yellow lichen bursts.
The washing hangs in fine catenary,
And chimneys disperse darkly-shredded smoke,
While out in Hartland Road when neighbours meet,
The day is ruled by fond belligerence.

The Terrace dominates the field of sight,
A polychrome outlook, hodgepodge design.
Hotels and guest houses are ranked in line,
In profile like a set of ragged teeth,
Bared 'gainst the Bay to challenge rage or still.

And all alone, across from Castle Rock,
High on the cliff with Shilling Stones below,
The red-brick vicarage holds fast the faith,
So redolent of smuggled wine and wreck,
Linked to the road by deeply rutted track,
Where worn stones rise to harness clay-slick pools.

The vicar, hastening from his sheltered church
(St Peter's is the name) ascends Back Hill
And cassock flapping braves the coastal track,
His figure cloaked in honest piety,
Gull shat upon despite a fervent prayer,
For gulls are no respecters of the cloth.

He looks towards Port Gaverne's eastern reach,
Where grassy Main goes fingering out to sea.
Into the Main, from foot of Headland's bluff,
A track incised by dint of Dartmoor's toil,
Grades gently down, the route for fine-split slates
Quarried at Welshman's, Tynes and Donkey's Hole,
Fetched in great wagon loads to reach the Main
And hauled on down to Gaverne's jetty prime
Carved clean from living rock to serve the ships
Which at high tide must bear the slates away.

Such slates were Gaverne's legacy and power,

And gift to Cornish folk and to the world.
Walls, roofs and lintels, flag-stoned kitchen floors
To serve through life, till at the bitter end
Comes fine-carved gravestone rich with homily.

The Main endures, firm in the ocean's thrall,
Grass-topped, cliff-rimed, sand-footed all about.
The sward worn smooth by tread of plimsolled feet
And blankets spread for picnics in the sun,
Ease-seeking during balm of summer days.

Dark caves and deeply sea-cut entrants scar
The Main imposing thick-cleft, slate-sheer flanks,
Its seaward end—a daunting precipice,
Where narrow gap defines the fabled Gut,
Deep water washing limpet-crusted rocks
Which anchor slippery hands of bladder wrack.

Across the Gut, rampart of Castle Rock
Rears hugely in its flat-topped majesty
On which sea pinks at random root and grip
In state of dogged fight against the odds.
Beyond this height doth Castle Rock make drop
To slow and gallant sea-blessed penitence.

At fall of tide do cormorants collect,
A clan mute and secure on weed-draped end.
Communal beaks are raised in full salute,
Awaiting fate to deal them half a chance
To sense a fish enveloped in the surge.
Between them strutting gulls hope entertain
With manner vacuous of stealing scraps.

Beach access from the top of sturdy Main
Is down into Tagg's Pit, steep steps, hand rail,
To reach the sun-decked rocks 'neath purple cliff.
Prismatic hole draws swimmers at high tide.
The beach at Tagg's is sandy, rock-pool girt
Where moles and bishops hide in greening weed,
And urchin spines test cowrie-hunting hands.

Not far without the lowest lap of tide,
Wave-rippled sand and kelp fields slickly brown
Drape meekly as they wait for rising flood
To once more liberate their flowing grace.

Across the way, a boldly verdant cliff
Of thrusting bluffs, high picket fence above,
Bites hard back at the Terrace and the hill
Down from Port Isaac—so behold Moon's Grave
Where death touched one whose resolution failed,
His story cherished is in legend's hand.

The sea holds calm behind, the sun delights.
Ascend Port Gaverne's damp and worm-cast beach
And tread the shingled shore where tank traps stood.
Now skimming stones abound and pebbles grind.

Along the high tide mark in ripe decay
Dark seaweed bank, the ardent gardener's gift,
Hosts hoppers, tiny crabs and cuttlefish,
And mermaid's purses thrown up by storm waves.

To left the jetty, gurgling stream on right
Emerges to fan wide from tunnelled course,

Its portal finely arched by mason's skill
Under the road that down from Headlands comes.

Steep-gullied 'gainst the Main and Annex heights,
Valerian and marguerites are spread
In grand profusion to bewitch the eye.
Valerian holds its fast-enduring grip
On meagre soil and thrives to win the day.

A dip at head of beach, and then the road,
O'er which spring tides invade with shingle grey,
Ascends anew to shake Port Gaverne free
And greet Port Isaac as a willing host
For Terraced guests and chance itinerants.

Facing the beach stand feathered tamarisks,
Fragrantly fine, free-whipping in the gale,
Pink blossoms subtle midst the pine-cast green.

For he who would his inner self refresh,
Strout's café glisters by the secret stream
In ivory trim, with bonhomie endowed.
The genial Mrs Strout dispenses tea,
In thick, chipped mugs, strong, steaming brown,
And coffee, Vimto, fancy cakes and splits
With jam and cream—if jam and cream there are.

Nearby for he whose taste to ale inclines,
The Port Gaverne Hotel boasts wholesome bar
Bedecked with portholes, craft of Granfer Jim
Whose garden graces valley bottom soil.
Behold the miracles his skill has wrought

And ponder on his calm magnificence.
Tobacco grows Jim in that dark, rich ground,
He cures and shreds it in his little shed
At seven Canadian Terrace on Fore Street
In Port Isaac below St Peter's church.

Aback the bar mine host purveys his brew,
Free-house refreshment to ignite the soul.
Granfer, whose palsied hand uncertain is,
Sips choice of draught through straw of hollow bone.

When summer fades, Port Gaverne folk are few
And furtive in their movements out of doors.
A cottage cluster here, another there,
White House, Pink House, the Bide-a-While hotel
And Cleave's farm outpost whereon valley folds
And gorse clad spurs and teeming bluebell woods
March firmly to Pendoggett's Cornish Arms.

Redundant cellars lie above the shore,
Square-blocked surround of crumbling courtyard walls,
The redolence of herring in the gloom
Drifts ghost-like in memoriam, glories past.

Without the cellars, firm in regiment
Until flat-roof clad house denies their march,
And stile to valley path must there be crossed,
Fine gardens thrive and beautifully flaunt
Their leguminous crop—potatoes, leeks,
Cabbage and turnip, parsnip, cauliflower,
Carrots and runners, cut-and-come-again,
Onions, broad beans and, over by a wall

To catch and hold the blessing of the sun,
Blackcurrant bushes drip with darkling fruit,
Strawberries crimson in a clean straw bed.
Mulched rare by sheep manure, tobacco plants,
Replete with promises of future smokes,
Are tended fair with gentle loving touch
And aid of seaweed carted from the beach.

All down the valley flows a stream. Its banks
Clay pocked and iris clad, and in its bed
There silt, here gravel, pothole, waterfall,
And he who dares can win the dust of gold
Diffused from discards up at Treore mine,
Which, while defunct, holds secrets sacrosanct.
There stood an engine house of laboured beam,
Cylinder straining o'er a furnace pit,
And brick-round chimney like a holy spire
To call the miners home. Its ruins stark
Hold still the thundering hymn of toiler's grace.

Better by far to seek the subtler gold
Of primrose sunburst nestled in a hedge,
Or, by a mighty trunk in elm tree's shade,
Before the bluebell lays its carpet down
In pallet to delight impressionist.

Astringent sloe and brown-shelled hazelnut
Are nature's harvest in the tangled woods,
And up on bracken-slopes and furze-clumped heath
From brambles droop the luscious blackberries,
A feast for heart and hand and home made pie
With apples plucked and sliced from cooker trees.

O'er valley swards do flop-humped rabbits lope,
Alert of ear, bob-tailed with lucky feet,
Preyed on by buzzard, ferret, gin and snare,
A cornucopia for man and beast.

As hill comes steeply down to Gaverne beach
From Cartway, must it make abrupt ascent
To gain Port Isaac's terraced bastion heights
Above the Moon's Grave picket sentinels,
Worn-weathered, grain-proud, shakily awry
By ledge-like walkway looking on the Main.
An apple tree, wind-shaped, its blossom sheds
In pink serenity at hill road's top,
Where halts the breathless traveller in relief.

The road goes on, the cliff path slips away
Downward and outward to the vicarage,
And Shilling Stones where adits three do gape
Linked to the cliff by slippery hand-hewn steps.
A coast-watch hut and coastguard station hold
In rapt attention scanning o'er the Bay,
Black canvas cone to hoist at gale's demand.

At Terrace start Bay View hotel resides,
There's Castle Rock hotel across the way,
Steadfast in hubris, pretence, vainglory.
And Tre-Pol-Pen, house-on-the-hill, the place
Where custom-tethered guests return to lodge
Who advent make by train, then bus (or car),
From Southern Railway at Port Isaac Road,
The station three miles out Pendoggett way.
The trains come down the line from Waterloo,

And on to Padstow, puffing through Wadebridge,
Where River Camel greets the shining tide.

Mark, as the Bay Hotel is passed on foot,
Tintagel Terrace coming from the left,
Its stony foot right-angling at the close,
Where face to face across the tarmac gulf,
That here is named New Road, reason obscure,
Two garages reek oil and vie for trade.

Resplendent on the right with pumps in front,
Famed far and wide for total excellence,
"Trelawney" dubbed, great hero, trusty hand,
Proprietors both marvels, brothers Prout,
Outlet for petrol, battery charge and car
Repairs. No job too small to undertake.
Oil furred inspection pit gapes in the floor
Darkly mysterious, a Hades gate.

The Prout Bros answer John and Mark by name.
Their management exudes an urbane charm.
Their mission—service to Port Isaac folk
Plus any others who might chance along
And drop in eager for transport somewhere.
For visitors who far would roam depend
On Prout's bus fleet, with first class guarantee—
Bedruthan Steps, or Bude and Clovelly,
Barnstaple, Bideford, serving Wadebridge
Through lanes made tight by burgeoning hedgerows.

Step forward ye who would loud praises sing
Of John and Mark and buses green and grey,

Of mystery tours to destinations strange,
Of schooldays there and back from Camelford,
Sir James Smith's Grammar School past Delabole.

Across the road the Central Garage sprawls,
Trelawney's rival, benign premises.
No buses there the way in do impede,
And men in once clean overalls do strive
To vent their skills on auto innocence,
While Mr Knight, Lancastrian when born,
Presides over his empire, noble, proud.

Yet two complete not garage paradise,
A third one falls in line—just over there
North Cornwall Transport stands, phone box beside.
In front three slender roads a nexus make—
There's New Road up to meet Trewetha Lane,
Where village dust is shaken from the feet,
Beyond stark council houses, blunt prefabs
And Hillson's farmyard slurried slick with rain.

Then Back Hill dropping into downtown's heart,
Direct through deep-cut banks with leafy fringe
Of evergreens; hard plodded, steep and true
By toiling feet, a stop midway for breath
To catch, and glance into the dark and dank
Of Bellevue Terrace, tight-mossed alleyway.

And Front Hill, graceful curve of slow descent
Past Church Rooms, rear of church and Hillson's Dump,
To meet Canadian Terrace, Chemist's shop
At Back Hill's foot, and so proceed beyond

Down Fore Street, place of shops and public house,
To terminus on Platt at harbour front.

North Cornwall Transport! Charlie Lobb's domain,
Where oil and water mix, and bold Bert Keat
Ploys shuffling travail in the stygian gloom.

About this complex hive of industry,
Twixt garage rear and coastguard's nether wall,
A great hall stretches in magnificence.
There every Friday night the public hies,
Eager for antique sights on sheeted screen.
Lined light projected through tobacco haze,
In glorious black and white and shades of grey,
By Mr Oliver, down-driven from St Teath.

The Rivoli! Bright jewel in Charlie's crown,
Fair cinema neath roof of galvanise.
The multitude files in and places takes,
Most regulars, few casual goers known.
Posteriors with gratitude are set
On dusty plush to while the hours away.
At front, dwarfed by screen, assemble boys
On wooden benches, splintery and hard,
Anticipating all that to them comes.

Old Rosie, eagle-eyed, alert to pounce
On miscreant and innocent alike.
To him they differ not, all ready game
For swift ejection as the serial starts.

"The Clutching Hand", "Flash Gordon" and "Tarzan",
Abbott, Costello, Hopalong and Fred

Astaire, epitome of style and grace,
(More loved than practised local qualities).
Hail Charlie, from whom countless blessings flow!

The exit weaves round corrugated sheets,
Close-in to left the coastguards gaily thrive
In station buildings looking on the Bay
From Varley's nose to far Tintagel Head,
Receivers of good wreck and easy times,
Marine custodians, constant diligence
For flotsam on the wave and public bar.

New Road before North Cornwall Transport lies.
It turns and climbs to wend its way towards
National Bus Garage, council house estate,
And divvy serving Co-op at hill crest,
Purveying groceries, fabrics, paraffin,
'Neath Mr Auger's eagle-vigilance.

Yet first, within stone's throw of Charlie's front,
Four-square behind a less than verdant yard,
Red steps lead up to Family Butcher's shop,
Proprietors are J N Hicks and Son,
Known in all walks and ways of Isaac's port.

The father John, and Jack his stolid son
In concert cleave at meat with expertise.
Brown Willy-profiled block, sawdusted floor,
And on a wall, network of gleaming tiles.
A beef side sways, suspended from a hook,
The fount of Sunday joints and pasty shins.
And John and Jack, prevaricators arch,
Duet as Sankey willed, in harmony.

From grizzled throats do pour such dulcet tones,
That customers are caused to quite forget
How rationing, scrag-end and drift of clock
Can lead to soporific timelessness.

Time marches slow and sure atop Front Hill—
In line of sight from singing butchers lair,
The Church Rooms weather slowly in their grounds.
There on a granite block with Celtic cross,
Rests list of hallowed names of those who fell
For king and country during two world wars,
Fourteen—eighteen, three-nine to forty five.
Honour is theirs, they are Port Isaac's pride,
Enshrined in memory each waking day.

Within the precincts of the Church Rooms dim,
Are great hall, ante-room and creaking stage.
A tea urn, radiant heat, fights winter chill,
Casting a spell when parish council meets
And public forum scorns its every wile.
Such rich debate spiced through with veins of wit,
A fitting match for "Worker's Playtime" best.

Through grimy panes of Church Room windows tall,
Light from without uncertainly doth break
To look on Front Hill, up which marked ascent,
On Poppy Day, from out the vestry door
Rod mounted cross is borne in process slow.
The cassocked choristers by vicar led,
Replete with ruff and surplice newly starched.

The bell above the vestry tolls its dirge,

Demanding monotone to summon all
Who to the church allegiance do own.
Matins, eleven, evensong at six,
With droning sermon, trumpet voluntary,
Church wardens ripe with pomp and piety.

Front Hill—an airy villa boulevard,
Guest house at top, small cottages behind.
Downhill a sweeping curve to meet Fore Street,
With Cliffside passage to the Hillson house
That looks across the Awn to Lobber Point
And down the Bay to Varley Head, where shade
From overhang conjures up canine eye,
As Head in sober sea-girt grandeur sleeps.

And there below 'gainst foot of crumbling cliffs,
Strong and secure, stalwart breakwaters cross
The Awn, enclosing inner harbour where
The waves run blunted and the fishing fleet
Tugs nervously at moorings thickly tarred.

Without the East breakwater, Hillson's Dump
Marks concave conduit twixt crest and beach.
From cliff top undeterred by wave and gale,
Domestic refuse, variegated full,
Is hove o'er edge to greet the cleansing tide
At height of flood, and, swallowed in the depths,
It is no more and perishes apace.

And daily come the folk to heave their loads
Down Hillson's Dump when rising tide permits.
Some furtive, some overt, yet equals all.

Diurnal Mr Hillson clumps en route
Up to his farm, high in Trewetha Lane,
To milk his kine and bear the milk in pails
To where the basins of his custom wait
All ready to be charged and placed on heat
To scald and liberate the golden cream.

At far side of the harbour throat the West
Breakwater bulks with bold impunity
'Neath Lobber cliff—though generations fade
This cliff is constant and implacable.
Although betimes comes fall of leafy slate
Excised by agencies of heckling gale
And winters grip when icicles hang large
From pendant ledges on the soaring face,
Traced fine by maidenhair and scurvy grass,
And subtle sea link bobs, with gull shit white
All fingering down to waken memories
Of Yuletide "Beano". See the jumbled rocks
Which Freddie trippled, fleet and sure of foot
On nimble toes to speed unto the heights,
Where wartime trenches festooned with barbed wire
Once ran like thunder to deter the Hun.
Now deep in brambles, yet they still survive
In silent tribute to victorious Port
And men whose courage conquered land and sea.

On seaward edge of Lobber Cliff there stands
A deeply hewn recess, cemented crusts,
Where brave men toiled apace upon a time
To lower concrete to the beach below.
Strong cables, block and tackle, fluid sacks,
To build breakwaters at the harbour gate.

To Lobber came the sacks across the fields,
With slushy concrete filled, a mighty load,
From road at Homer Park atop Church Hill,
Down hedge-trapped rutted lane, by name
Of Washing Pool, under the wind and larks.
Some concrete set, avoiding destiny.
The solid sacks were builded into walls,
And are there yet, stark white against the thorns,
The ghosts of hessian rough upon their form.

Nor wind, nor time, nor shade of Lobber's frown
Could still construction of the monoliths—
Both West and East breakwaters tapered rise,
Great parapets to dull assaulting waves
That would do harm to foreshore's shingled slope
And fishing fleet moored tight upon the tide.

Set then your back to Hillson's dump and gaze
At noble grace of Fore Street's gentle slope,
Slow slipping from Front Hill to Town Platt verge,
Where lifeboat slipway glides by cobbled Lake
To wash the beach from out of valley's depth.
There Pawlyn's cellars rests in noisome pride
Twixt Lake and 'Skarrock Hill and Lobber path.

The scene harks fair, Fort Street in summer's prime,
Flowing with visitors and Flora dance.
In winter's grey a gun might well be fired
From Back Hill's foot towards Victoria House,
And ball with living soul would ne'er collide.
In such drear days Fore Street's aspect is bleak.
(A blessing then—in Delabole 'tis worse).

Dear Back Hill rises like an arrow's flight,
Foot ruler straight, steep run trajectory
To slow the pace of feet that agile were
On Fore Street. Challenge then Back Hill—
A daunting task—ye faint of heart bear right
By Mine Pit Corner at the rusting pump,
And take for gentleness Trewetha Lane
If you would Co-op gain with strength intact.

To left of Mine Pit stands St Peter's church,
Magnificent upon its terraced height.
A pathway paved leads up to the church door,
Commanding myriad of slated roofs,
Khandallah, far Church Hill and Lobber Cliff,
And cry of gulls on telegraph poles perched.

Between Back Hill and church imposing front
A mineshaft capped by ancient rotting planks
Is lodestone grandly set for eager boys
Released from Sabbath trial by Sunday school,
Made numb by pious teacher's ritual cant,
With censure fresh for unremembered text,
(Strange bedfellows are boys and piety).
They race without the church and hurdle wall
To leap and prance on shaft's uncertain cap,
And relish sound of errant tumbling stones,
Echoing deep, below their best-shod feet,
A hundred feet or more to adit drear
Where ochred walls weep outwards to the cave
Whose gash divides East breakwater from school.

St Peter's lives in state upon Back Hill.
No spire or steeple mars its princely form.

West of Castle Rock

Barn-like, its lichened roof cascades slick slates
To rusted gutters, moss choked, grass festooned,
O'er gothic windows mullioned front and side,
Lead tracery refined upon blind glass.
Yet at the rear, bright images hold sway,
Christ on the cross triumphant centrepiece.

Within the church soft quietude prevails.
Stone walls shed steady chill upon the nave,
Where row on row of woodworm'd chairs provide
Scant comfort for the congregation's zeal.
Two chairs are marked by crisply regal staves.
There sit church wardens, men of destiny,
No strangers they to parsimonious hearts.
See how they pace the nave, all measured tread
With velvet bags to snare the widow's mite.

The nave breaks at three steps, a railed way
To pulpit, sanctuary and choir stalls,
And altar, organ pipes and gleaming brass,
With entry way at right from whence the choir
In tuneless mien the vestry fug vacates.
Service is born—and down there in the nave
The congregation proves Chrysostom's prayer.
Then praise the Lord, with hymn and psalm and chant!
Bless opening time that Evensong succeeds.

The low retaining wall at church west edge,
Slate peaked, cascades profuse valerian blooms,
To terraced gardens at its foot, alive
With tetties, carrots, beets and curly greens.
There black-clad elders till the heavy soil
And sit in sheds, sequestered at the wall.

They dream of ships which sailed in days of yore,
Till dinner time mandates return to hearth.

Below, joined cottages, gull-spattered slates,
Chimneys investing soot into the air,
Thus spotting washing draped on sagging lines,
And speckling whitewash crusted on the walls.
Combined, Canadian Terrace they become—
At number seven live Granfer and Gran,
And in the front bedroom of number six,
In nineteen thirty-nine a child was born
To Bill and Betty. He now pens these words.
On their beloved lives the sun has set,
As on so many who Port Isaac made
Their memory endureth like the rock,
Leaf-slated flags and granite crystal-bright.

Canadian Terrace smiles its weathered face
On gardens front, no vegetables there:
Perhaps a strip of euphemistic lawn
Dun-faded, bordering on wallflower beds,
Snapdragon, primrose and forget-me-not,
Wild garlic rampant drift, invading mint.

Worn steps descend to Fore Street. Once there, lo,
The corners of Back Hill are boldly pinned
In place by chemist's shop and Liberal Club.
Across the way, sunk firm beside the cliff,
The Primary school, all clamour at playtime,
Eternal, resolute with classes four.
Wind-fretted sandstone cornices prevail
While clot-starred cream of local youth attend.
Come sleet, come snow, come fog, come driving rain,

To school they trudge in hobnail booted ranks,
Down from the hills; the farms and valleys out,
By duty bound and threat of chastisement.

Let glit'ring prize not mar their aptitude,
Let halls of academe their feet ignore,
Let study not disturb their daydreams fair,
Let dullard's dues their waking thoughts imbue.
Time's patient flow will bear them from the dark
To dawn of disillusion's disarray.

They are as one, this primary entourage,
Accented tongues, scabbed knees and penury,
Their unity steeped in Port Isaac's soul,
To do or die and strive against the odds.

Young villagers of more refined mien,
(And means), to private Terrace school repair,
There to avoid the great unwashed contact—
Their stool, for all that, reeks in manner like.

Twice daily playtime comes, one quarter hour
When playground doth erupt, anarchy rules,
Mad football rages up and down the court,
And here and there a fight attracts a crowd.
Upon a risen knoll by Lifeboat House,
Girls, skipping ropes, flash knickers navy blue.

At close of play assembly lines must form,
Ranked as to class, held ramrod straight in line
By Boss's flick'ring cane. When order reigns,
The files on shuffling feet to class proceed.
Boss, blessed Head, a Brylcreemed martinet

Who binds school spirit with authority,
Hand dulcet set about by forged glove
In iron pure, sharp moulded for respect.

From school some boys hare fast to chemist's shop
Where Mrs Cowling garishly presides.
Behind cosmetic mask there lurks a smile,
Dispenser of sweet ration and ice cream,
And pharmaceutical medicaments.
Her husband Lynwood wisely biding time.
Glimpsed hovering in back near kitchen door.

Above the entry port these words are writ—
"The Old Drug Store" in Olde English script,
So that "Old Drug Score" seemeth there to be.
Beware ye now, for Mrs Cowling hath
Betimes good days, when generosity
No limit takes in extra measure's weight
Full plumb upon the scales. Yet bad days come
To render customer more wrong than right,
For then her tongue doth lash the innocent.

By Fore Street entry door to chemist's shop,
On cushion rests an evil Pekinese
In corpulent abandon, feigning sleep.
Billy by name, he holds himself in wait
To yip and snarl, at passing ankles snap,
And Mrs Cowling's approbation gain.
A well aimed foot may Billy's pomp deflate,
Then wrath of Mrs Cowling in full flood
Engendered is, and miscreant had best
To heeled flight repair and go to ground.

Look up! There on a bluff of weathered slate,
Dust-sifting down to Back Hill foot below,
Bedecked on high with pink-wisped tamarisk
Stands Doctor's house and cosy surgery,
Where come the multitude to squander time
And trust in physic brown and green and white
To liberate imaginary ills,
And voice complaints to ever-willing ears
Of those arrayed in state around the walls.

In inner sanctum Doctor Sproull presides.
Proceed with hope all ye who enter there!
His healing hands do evenly dispense.
Wise counsel soothes his anxious clientele.
His word his bond, beloved by one and all.
The weak are soothed—malingerers beware!

Of such great men brave songs are loudly sung.
His magnitude is equal to his fame,
And pillared firm with Boss the Headmaster,
And Atterbury-Thomas Reverend,
With Mr Pearce, policeman of the Port,
Authority's umbrella spreads supreme.
We praise and honour these as men of men,
Custodians of village circumstance,
Quelling disquietude with clip to ear,
For boys who miss the straight and narrow way
Are legion, be of that assured.
They toe no line with spirits unconfined.

The stately tread of Mr Pearce bears down,
Yet troublemakers flee not from his sight,

Accepting justice as he metes it out,
His iron will in rustic moleskin clad,
As soft as velvet forked from hummocked ground,
And fair as sunset over Varley Head.

Ye men of greatness, tell, where are you now?
Tom Brown, old Nibs and Jess and Ningy Short,
And Charlie Lobb, dear Rosie and John Neal,
Sweet, Honey, Hills and Glover, May and Steer,
And Hicks and Prout, and Provis, Saundry, Short,
Thomas and Oaten, Hosking, Masters, Keat,
Scott, Robinson and Sherratt, Rowe and Cann—
Blest families who to this Port belong.
Their hallowed names resound in every stone,
And grace the walls on which their shoulders leaned.
In shadow-dappled corners live they yet.

Though' rogues there were among this favoured host,
Time's harrow hath smoothed fine their furrowed ways.
In peace they rest, in memory revered.
Blithe characters who quipped their path through life.
Refined in wit, to fortune hostages,
Denied the step to goals that were their right.

They were and are the Port, their spirits slip
In Middle Street along the coursing Lake,
On Town Platt, strait Rose Hill, the harbour beach,
In Dolphin Street, on gradient of Church Hill.
Roscarrock Hill, New Road, Trewetha Lane
And Lobber's verdant swards have known their tread
In hobnail-studded soles and rough sea-boots.
Then Long Pool, Search'ry Gug and Plaice Pool sand,

Breakwaters, Boney's Castle and Pink Pool,
Were theirs to cherish, water, mirror bright,
Absorbed their forms and held them to itself.

Yet, stand we still at Fore Street's gracious peak
Abaft the Liberal Club, eyes firmly set
To course on down to Chapman's, Little Hill
With public toilets hard against the cliff.
We there below find barber William John;
Tair Bunt the fruiterer; the Pentice wall;
The Post Office, aura of rectitude;
The Golden Lion, spilt bitter redolence;
And Sherratt's at the side in Stanley House
Where bread fresh-baked enhances daily life,
And splitters, soft yeast buns and saffron cake
Delight perfection-seeking connoisseurs.
On outer corner, in Victoria House,
Greengrocer's trade is vigorously plied.
Inside the bend, newsagent Mrs Rowe
Lines up bright comics for the eager boys.

A step or two and Fore Street is soon done.
A chip shop beckons on the narrow way,
And Mrs Keat, brow gleaming by the fryer,
Drops lengths of battered fish in bubbling lard,
Then hauls them out again, crisp, golden brown.

From canyon dark Fore Street emerges free
Upon the Town Platt, Wheelhouse on one flank,
And Pawlyn's cellars looms on far side's edge,
A bastion twixt Lake and 'Skarrock Hill.

Aback, the stately walled-in Slipway court—
Hotel and bold Black Doors are framed about
By Lake and Middle Street and Church Hill's foot.
And then the Harbour Café, mystic site,
Its whitewash peeling in the harbour breeze.
Mine host within serves Künzles, tea and wit,
A peerless man whom bullshit hath embraced
And taken for its own. A prince of men!

Thus have we traversed Fore Street, end to end,
And on the way, with skimpy strokes endowed
Our precious canvas with a structured soul.
Now seeks the landscape details in to fill,
Ensuring character in colours bold.

To Liberal Club we then return to daub
Strokes grandiose in red and yellow hue,
Rememb'ring Dingle Foot transformed to red.
No politicians now! Endeavour thus
In monosyllables the time of day
To pass with they who come to frame the balls.
On snooker table great their skills to flaunt
As if Joe Davis had inspired their cues.

Along the walls, the idle sit in line.
See rising from them, a tobacco haze
Invading rafters browning high above.
Spittoon, strategic placed, appears well missed.
In honoured spot a crafted scoreboard shines,
Bearing the name of Castle, L.E.V.,
Born to be great, that baize-encumbered knight
Whose rotund form bestrode the splintered floor,
His liberal hand in a Churchillian glove.

Before the fireplace, aged oil stove fumes,
And at a table, dominoes and cards
Click, slap and slide on patina of grime.
Old Freddie, the bucolic concierge
Of Club and precincts, dentures gripping pipe,
Dust coat and trilby hat in timeless style,
History large writ on shoulders passing broad—
Though' marked by age, yet youthful is his gait.
In mind's eye Freddie walks forever hale,
Dispensing warmth to all who *bon mots* crave.
His character doth surely bless the Club,
Recipient of awe from membership.
Founded the Club nineteen-eleven was.
O, then stood Freddie in his lusty prime,
And his bold spirit now anoints the hall.

Set down the chalk, release the sterile cue!
Let willing feet wend down to Little Hill,
Where benches stretch to ease the gossip's beat!
There o'er the harbour, look to 'Skarrock Hill,
And feast the eyes on mansions there arrayed—
Khandallah resting fair in Lobber's arms,
Allotments sweep in columns at its verge.
Wind-tortured poplars and sweet withies rise
By Roy May's quarry grey-hewn in the hill
And muddy path to tramp down to Port Quin.

Roy's house is high upon a terrace placed.
Of visage grim, it menaces the Port.
Northcliff stands tall, vertiginously set.
Tucked in behind, cottage of Teddy Bush
Sleeps unaware that future fame awaits
Tenure of haemophobe practitioner.

At Little Hill we sit and calmly gaze
O'er wall, valerian decked, which marks cliff edge.
From benches poised we benefit from sun
That in its heaven doth soak the harbour tight.
On left the public lavatories adjoin
A dumping chute to gug throat underneath,
Where ground sea winnow may a black coin sort
From tramp iron, rusty nails and barrel hoops.

To lavatories the desperate bend their steps,
Relief for breaking necks and needy peers.
Fine words on walls indelibly inscribed
Will justify the penny cost to read.
Forbidden fruit these words to curious boys,
Whose evensong collection opens doors
For "comfortable one" (as quoth old Jess
At parish meeting, accent raucous, bold).
Rear ends in place within o'erhang the tide,
The written words delight the questing gaze.

Above a cobbled stretch great rolling doors
As red as rust stand tall, and broader yet,
Beflanked by granite pillars, steadfast, true.
The school gate holds them out upon the left.
The grand lifeboat, which once behind those doors
Found respite pending call to brave the deep,
And ride the storm's hard edge and peril brace,
Atlantic rage to vanquish, souls to save.
It shot the slipway, paved with village heart,
Washed with the blood of princely lifeboat men
Who ruled the waves as lions, fearless hearts
Instilled with sacred maxim "One and All".

On Little Hill the gossips sit and yarn
Away the hours of God's soft daylight good.
No one can move on Lobber Field but he
Be seen and fast dissected as a knave
By restless tongues that eager are for fuel.
No lady fair can to her stall devolve
And miss a flight of well-fletched arrow words
Aimed at her back, aspersions jocular.
No shopper, penny-counting, Chapman's bound,
Can fail to have her errand questioned deep.
For here on Little Hill no knife is sheathed
When vulnerable backs present themselves,
And barbs as fine as sit on fishing hook
Are cast at will to wound the uninvolved,
In line with gossip rules, or so say they.

In Chapman's, just downhill, the shelves are stocked
With biscuit tins, fish paste jars and baked beans.
On marbled top resides a mighty cheese
Beside a block of butter, pats in place.
The bacon slicer winds a razor gleam
As deft peeled rashers fall to Jack's true hand,
A gift for eggs in hope yet unfulfilled.
The jocund staff do rationing belie,
'Neath counter top do lurk clandestine goods
Awaiting onset of the favoured few.

Then Mr Hillman, dapper, blazer clad,
Slick manager from somewhere up the line,
Applies his wide boy patter of renown.
He boldly leadeth from the very front,
A vibrant MC at the Temperance Hall

Who audience cajoles in heart and voice
To sing as rivals 'cross the no-man's aisle.
One side gives vent to "Tipperary" strain.
"Pack up your troubles" soars over the way.
A truce is called, with declaration firm
That all have won, and concert may commence.

A few steps down from Chapman's; on the right,
A door discreet reveals a narrow hall
To sanctuary holy to the male,
Wherein snips William John at barber's trade.
Short back and sides, a little off the top,
His clippers clog on surfeit of Brylcreem.
A shave perhaps, a dabble of Bay Rum,
And something for the weekend emphasised.

See William John, urbane and dignified,
In ambling shuffle over hair-strewn floor.
A joke, a quip, advice, informed debate
With customers tight crowded all around.
A mirror crazed reflects the cosy scene.
Through salty panes the lilting harbour sleeps.

A score—no more—of paces confident
Down, down, twixt cottages whitewashed,
And slate flagged steps to sombre, frowning doors,
To Pentice wall on which to lean and view
The harbour beach and rise of 'Skarrock Hill,
The chapel at its foot, o'er Pawlyn's glimpsed.

The Pentice roof, gull-scrabbled, sitting steep
On rank of fisher cellars, time-worn doors,
Tar-streaked and spattered footing, crab pots piled.

The "Golden Lion" crowns the lower end
Of Pentice wall's smooth crown-slick patina
That generation's arms have laid and left.
Well-loved scene to admire as gossip flows,
As e'er it must on Fore Street's winsome way.

The shop that looks towards the Pentice wall,
Fruiterer is, proprietor A. Bunt.
The "A" means Altair, ("Old Tair" to the boys)
Who daily hone his patience wafer thin,
Yet never dent his keen parsimony.
Farewell Old Tair, no tick here, mark thee well,
Let Pentice stones absorb thy memory,
And candles, matches, brown-crabbed apples sharp
Support thy ear-ringed slouch 'neath khaki coat.
Before thee at the wall men stand in line,
Backs to thy face, arms folded fast to slate.
This grand commune a message sublimates,
Below its feet the fisher's cellars reek
Of tar and 'bacca, salt and withies green.

On crest of Town Platt, metronomic pace
Of ancient mariners who gladly march
In unison—ten paces to the turn;
Ten paces fro, no army better drilled.
They talk of sea-boots, ships and dinner time,
Yarns spun in discord, tall as Lobber cliff,
With puff of pipes and viscid cheek-stuffed chaws.
An endless walk, with destination void.

From fount of Pentice wall dear Fore Street falls,
In gentle solitude through canyon tall.
The buildings crowd in tight from either side,

And commerce beckons all whom errands run—
There's Post Office, pub, baker, greengrocer,
Newsagent and chip shop to Town Platt's edge.

Betimes the lifeboat plied this narrow way,
Tight-hauled by men of Guernsey-shrouded steel,
Whose essence rests in every blessed thread
The fabric of the Port doth constitute.

Post Office then, there over on the left,
Its precincts with integrity imbued.
The décor smacks of harsh austerity.
No comfort here to pass the time of day.
The smell of ink, a counter painted brown,
Tall altar to the god of postage stamps.
The business runs with zeal of martinet,
A letter registered, post order crisp.
All equal they who dare to enter here
The bureaucratic soul to homage pay.

Yet fear not! Creaking in the crafty breeze
The pub sign "Golden Lion" gently swings,
Inviting all who thirst for greater things
To come within and slake their keen desires
In public forum, sawdust on the floor.
From out the bar flat-tapped St Austell ales,
A thud of darts which doubles vainly seek,
A haze of smoke, a dearth of intellect.

Beyond the pale the saloon bar awaits
Sports jackets, green cravats and accents clipped,
Gin-sipping toffs over the great divide

Which pens the rank and file where they belong.
Like church and chapel, ne'er the twain shall meet.

St Austell ales! The house is firmly tied,
Mine host dispenses to his clientele.
The door catch snickers as they come and go
With ITMA regularity to bladders void.

Thus Fore Street slips away as in a dream,
A perfect bend, the Town Platt within sight,
A curve held fast in place by Sherratt's shop,
Rowe's Newsagent's and Jim's greengrocery.

Tangential to the bend a way, tight, strait,
Heads unto Dolphin Street through Temple Bar,
With rugose floor, its shoulder-burnished walls
Restrict the muscle-bound and corpulent.

Sherratt's the bakers, splits and crusty bread,
Yeast buns, jam pasties, golden saffron cakes
Lined up on racks, delectable and fresh,
Warm to the touch, a blessing to the taste.
And weekly comes a famous pasty batch
To which the multitude flock eagerly.

And Mrs Sherratt, mobile poetry,
Her presence bustling, energetic, kind.
Praise to the Sherratts, touched by hand of God.
Their heavenly bread doth feed us evermore.

On outer corner stands Victoria House,
Where jolly greengrocer his trade doth ply—

Cox apples, cookers, names to conjure with,
Potatoes, greens and vegetables arrayed.

Yet none so firm as roots which on the cart
Of brothers Blake doth wend Port Isaac's ways.
Loud "Turnips, cabbage!" chants their harbinger.
Men of the soil, Trewetha on their boots,
And in their eyes a vision of the plough
Whose razored furrows draw a wake of gulls
To shining earth and plodding, trusty horse.

The inner corner boasts the newsagents,
Interior gloom lit up by newsprint page.
The daily news is topically purveyed,
Here "Sketch", there "Mirror" and News Chronicle",
With "Beanos" lying out in regal state,
Each one emblazoned with subscriber's name
In blue-black ink, by Mrs Rowe's fair hand.
Her bird-like frame contains an iron core
Round heart of gold to bless each customer.

Yet he who would the Sunday sheets inspect,
Avid to read of vicars compromised
By incidents where intimacy occurred,
Must head to friendly roadside parking spot
Where Bill Melhuish from his car boot deep
Draws "People", "Dispatch" and "News of the World"
To satisfy each hidden instinct base
And tablecloth create for coming week.

As Fore Street sheds its final score of yards
To greet the Town Platt by the Wheelhouse front,
One gem remains in this deep, sunless way.

On plate glass window condensation creeps,
Chips tumble in their wells of seething lard,
While on a shelf lie golden battered fish
Congealing fat pooled white in trough below.

A perfect newsprint square, a skilful fold,
A cone is formed in which are placed the chips,
And on them sprinkled vinegar and salt
With liberal hand, so never quite to taste.
O manna! Fish and chips and Mrs Keat,
To thee we bow our heads eternally.
Thy product doth beguile the inner man.

To Fore Street a reluctant back we set.
Its charm will linger long to thrill the soul.
We set our feet on Town Platt's hoary stage
In front of Middle Street and great Black Doors.
The Harbour Café windows, tight and quaint,
The Wheelhouse tow'ring up to gull-peaked roof,
The hauled-up punts, the crab pots piled awry,
Thick-rusted anchor and deltaic Lake.

And there the shingled beach, the sand, the sea,
The pulsing tide the harbour doth anoint,
And benediction lap on weed-fringed rocks
Where mussels cling and limpets gently graze.

And shingle shelves up to the dark recess
Where Searchery Gug, axe-sharp, cuts Lobber Cliff.
The tortured blackthorn, woven by the gale
Defines allotments barren upper tithe.

To left we turn and gaze where Pawlyn's wall

Obtusely darts to Halwyn's 'Skarrock steps.
A lower gate defies the rising tide
To wash its foot and billow in the yard,
Or crash in mighty gug 'neath Halwyn's tower,
Recesses softly dark, clean smell of weed,
A candle needed there to penetrate
Below Roscarrock Hill in dripping depths.

Then rock-strewn rippling sand, an ample pond
Wherein plaice nestle, tiny, camouflaged.
Bare toes can seek them out with sense of squirm.

Allotments grip the concave cliff above,
Their debris spilling arbitrarily,
For tide to bear away on trusted ebb.
Go tripple o'er the rocks, dry dormancy,
The drooping bladder wrack, slick-shiny, brown,
Keen for the flood, its resurrection sure.

There at the verdant curve of Lobber cliff,
The rising field that sweeps up to the crest
Where slender trenches Home Guard presence knew,
The rugged face of bristling slate appears.
And giant jumbled boulders, shades of grey,
Lie at the foot of tow'ring precipice
And pin back slope of sliding, shifting scree
Long fallen from the heights and crags above,
Ledge course and fearsome gulf that Lobber is.

The western breakwater can scarce contain
Its tenuous grip on Lobber's sundered base.
It thrusts its battered bulk against the sea,

West of Castle Rock

No ebb too low to leave its walls unwashed.
Black Annies stand on crusted battlement
To strut and test the wind with raucous bills.
From rust-caked metal tower, light's steady pulse
Complies with harbourmaster's cursive eye
And metronomic kelp in current's grip.

Across the harbour see the pendant School,
See Long Pool sprouting heads of lobster pots—
Great withy stores replete with shellfish charge.
In this one lobsters, in another crabs,
Brown waiters bound to gourmet palate grace.
See Boney's Castle under Little Hill,
Whose ledges at high tide make swimmer's dream,
With path vertiginous to gain the school,
Handholds to tempt the bold and test the brave.

The harbour! Was there e'er a sight so fair
To charm both villager and visitor?
This wondrous spot, in ebb or at the flood,
Its timeless beauty revels in each gale
That tears the spume from curling crest of wave.
And in the calm, the sparkle of the tide,
Each precious ripple sound as girding cliffs,
And peerless yet as Lobber Point's dark wedge
That rides Atlantic run at Awn's deep gate.

Across the Slipway where the fragrant Lake
'Neath Fore Street runs in darkened solitude,
The doors to Pawlyn's cellars welcome friends
To solace seek in inner courtyard's peace,
Suffused with sanctity and ripening fish,

Tar, withy wands and sawdust crisply dry.
Dark nets adorn the inner walls, or lie
In neat profusion on the chaw-stained floor,
From Bark House brought, up in old Dolphin Street,
Trevan House neighbour, nearby Temple Bar.

Half finished crab pots drape from template heads,
And withy cuttings litter the surrounds.
A school of gurnards fester in a tank,
These bait will form to prove a lobster's taste
When fixed in pots and on sea bottom laid.

Yea! Pawlyn's verily forms vibrant base
For fisher fleet that braves the tossing deep
To ride grey waves out in the daunting Bay.
"Eternal Father", let our voices raise,
Our brethren shield in this our mortal hour.

In Pawlyn's Tom Brown's word equates with law.
No silver star adorns his Guernsey blue
As tall he stands, saddled authority.

Stand then in Pawlyn's portal—see Church Hill
Climb upwards to the heights, grade one in five.
It lies ahead and with its gentler start
By Slipway House, its steepness is belied.
Church Hill ascends to rolling hinterland
Past Homer Park, Trefreock nestling calm
In sheltered hollow where the sweet well springs
And runs its stream through deep banks to Pine Awn.

Across the fields, a bridle path defined
By generations' feet on hallowed sward,

To tramp to St Endellion past Pennant
And reach the church of unimagined age.
Of granite built, its battlemented tower
Commanding view of Cornwall north and south.
And there below, the tombstones ranked in rows,
Some leaning, foundered under blows of time.
Yet mark they places where in memory dear
Port Isaac's saints and knaves reside in peace.
For all are equal in Endellion's ground.

Above the Slipway House by red phone box,
A butcher's shop welcomes its chosen folk.
No Sankey gems are rendered in this one—
Pure business in the order of the day.
There may be beef or lamb or rosy pork,
And sausages and brawn and hog's pudding
To tempt the shopper—given luck of course.

Off a small courtyard on the other side,
The cobbler sits, his last industrious.
Fine leather shards raise incense at his feet
As hobnails enter soles in patterns gay.

Ascend Church Hill perchance but fifty yards—
The path into the valley joins the road.
It points its muddy course at valley depths
Past gardens, watercress and Old Mill House,
Where once the huge wheel yielded to the race
That down from grand Mill Pool did madly surge
When opened sluice gate freed torrential flow.

The Mill Pool tranquil spreads—within its swamp
Do grow the willow stumps, the fisher's prize,

Forth casting myriad of withy wands,
The bounty nature gives at break of spring.

To left of withy stand the path turns up
Through hazel, elder, bramble and blackthorn,
To reach Trewetha via Archer Farm,
Precarious gates and barns with sagging roofs.

Two streams do at the Mill Pool head unite—
The one doth wend its way down from Frogpool,
Colstanton Corner, Poltreworgey Hill,
And road beyond from grim-faced Delabole.
The other rises near Tresungers Farm,
Old manor house with ne'er a serf in view.
It flows beneath Pennant, Seven Acres field
Alive with blackberries in autumn sun.

Beside this stream, protected by barbed wire,
Tom Saundry's orchard, trunks in lichen clad,
With cooking apples born to grace a pie
Fit for the table of the best and least,
On sale in Tom's small shop in Middle Street
Beside the channelled Lake's quick babbling flush.

Walk to the sacred top of Middle Street,
Past Manor House and pump and Poor Court yard,
Where tight Back Alley climbs up to Rose Hill,
Allotments pinned to slope by ivied walls.

There Wesley Chapel, brick built, calm, austere,
Firm in the valley holds God's ground intact.
It welcomes mammon through its hallowed doors,
With gusto rendering their favourite hymns,

Then from the pulpit local preachers rail
'Gainst strong drink, church and lapse of godliness.

Of chapels in Port Isaac are there two.
One under God, opponents in His name.
Ecumenism is considered not.
Fine folk do suspect tolerance display.

The second smoulders on Roscarrock Hill,
Its gauntlet down by Pawlyn's back wall thrown.
Its congregation, pious and devout,
Flock to the pews to seek the Lord's good grace,
Their presence sure for roll up yonder call.

Above the chapel, hill's rain-rutted rise
Points squarely at the ways down to Port Quin.
Ascend ye 'Skarrock hill to greet Northcliff,
Where grove of tortured poplar trees defends
Khandallah's ramparts, and the path induce
To fork—one branch to right doth rise
To Lobber field by the allotments head.
It rambles onwards down the crinkled coast
To traverse Kellan Head and touch Port Quin.

The destination of path branching left
Is Port Quin too, yet on a shorter cut
That sweeps o'er hill and dale, and on its way
Dips through Freak valley, streaming to Pine Awn.
The deep-cut channel crossed on slated bridge,
'Neath twisted willows, riven by the wind.

Upon the further slope primroses glow,
And light the hillside midst the bracken tall,

Soon to surrender to the bluebell flush,
A carpet azure, shifting in the breeze.

This pathway moves on to Roscarrock Farm,
And gently slips o'er stiles and mushroomed grass
Grazed tight by rabbits, (legion is their host),
Down to Port Quin, declining there below,
A place of blight, a godforsaken hole
Without a cinema, sans joy, sans life.

A road winds in, climbs up and out again.
Dead cottages decay in ivied line.
Their roofs have long succumbed to time's neglect.
No doors are there protecting hearth and home,
The lintels sag, the stones dissociate,
And nettles congregate on weathered mounds.

From tangled damsons and a creaking pump,
The road down to the sea front darkly falls,
The harbour rocky, open to the Bay,
The Cow and Calf, foam girded in the swell,
And Doyden squatting on its sea-pinked Head.

The path from Lobber curves past Lobber Point,
To reach Pine Awn through honeysuckled gorse,
And brambles drooping fruit on every side
For traveller to pluck to speed his way.

A waterfall spills clean onto the beach
In Pine Awn's shingled cove—the dusty way
Ascends the daunting hill, a test for feet,
And aching calves and stops to gather breath.

At last the top, and displayed far below
In all its rocky glory, Crowser cove.
A pair of ravens launch from sheltered ledge
In croaking circles, Crowser's royalty.

Look north along the sweep of grey-hazed cliffs
Tintagel Head, Trebarwith, Donkey's Hole,
Bounds Cliff, St Illick's Well and Tartar Cove,
The cowslipped Welshman's Quarry, Grandma's Chair,
Great heights of slate, bedecked by raucous gulls,
Black Annies, razorbills and guillemots,
And kittiwakes, dark shags and cormorants.
Poised bills, on water's edge they ruminate,
And eye the deep for fish among the kelp.
Then Cartway Cove, just where this tale began,
Around to Castle Rock, Port Gaverne strand,
The Terrace at hill top and Lobber's rim.

All this the ravens spy with lazy glance,
A rising eddy lifts their sombre wings.
They drift round to the left, and there they see
The Rumps at western limit of the Bay—
The horn-set Rumps there snuffling at the sea
As if to bite Mouls Island's greening cone,
A pivot in the cusp of Lundy Bay.

Past Crowser Island, sea stack at low tide,
To golden sands that rest in Varley's lee.
On then to Kellan Head by Foxhole Rocks,
Indomitable bulwark, gale-honed grass,
Where once coast watcher's hut stood bluntly proud,
Intrepid vigil, guardian of the Bay.

On Gaverne Beach

Port Quin in sight, its harbour mute below.
At journey's end we bless the constant cliffs.

Then let us stand again on Lobber Field!
The bounding hill, Khandallah at our feet,
'Neath azure skies the green sward's glory set,
Alive with pink-tipped daisies to be plucked
And chained to grace the necks of dalliants.
We marvel at the Port and valley deep,
Blue ridges that recede towards Pennant,
The clustered roofs that stagger o'er downtown,
The harbour bright, the little bobbing boats,
The Town Platt, Church Hill's lark-like rise,
Whose song enriches St Endellion's gate
And ground where rest our ever-blessed sons,
The best, the worst, beloved or reviled.
At journey's end in hallowed soil they lie.
There stands the school, against the cliff edge sheer,
With steep Back Hill behind, Port Gaverne bound.

God bless this jewel in dear North Cornwall's crown,
Revere its stones, the slates that make it whole,
Heap praises on its folk, its character,
Its whimsies and traditions, fishermen
And farmers, labourers, may grace be theirs,
And peace descend upon the indolent.

Port Isaac is and was, and e'er shall be.
Let we who are of it suffuse with pride,
And lift our hearts to sea-girt paradise.

Castle Rock and the Port Gaverne Main

3

On Gaverne Beach

The ebb has flowed its course; the beach at Gaverne
Holds grateful strangers cherished by the sun
Upon the slope in Tagg's Pit's gentle haven;
Down on the sand undulate ripples run.

No curling waves break white on Castle Rock;
Today the Gut is still—in lucent deep
Stir slowly fronds of kelp on rooted block
As dainty unseen currents gently creep.

From Main grass, springy, finely draw and stiff,
To blowhole, fault and ever-beckoning cave,
Across the beach the overhanging cliff
Casts shadows long far down into Moon's Grave.

The foreshore, tide-tossed crunching shingle bank,
Bold jetty, slate-carved terrace in its prime,
The kipper cellars, cob-walled file and rank
Sad victims are of melancholic time.

And yet in Gaverne, levity full grown—
Marks hostelry set bold above the leat,
Green Door Club, Bide-a-While stand not alone;
Strout's Café, sandwiches with potted meat.

The long, slow hill that to Port Isaac leads:
Set Gaverne to the back and upward plod
To summit where the high-born Terrace bleeds
In praise of mammon in full gaze of God.

The Port Isaac Terrace and Moon's Grave

4

The Terrace

Seen from afar, its prospect could not be finer!
It looks as boldly impregnable as the Great Wall of China.
Its dark magnificence bestrides the Gaverne crest.
Come, nervous traveller, be welcomed as a guest.

Seen closer to, its prospect is even more of a blessing.
Indeed it would not be difficult to call it quite prepossessing,
Houses tight in line, as if designed by a committee.
With the presence of hotels adding lustre to the kitty.

A hotel and then a guest house, and next a private dwelling
If there is any difference between them, no one is really telling.
The visitors stay for a fortnight and appreciate full board,
Never absent at the moment the afternoon tea is poured.

A simple track of access runs before the Terrace row,
Full wondrous is the vista it embraces down below-
A sweeping panorama of Port Gaverne and the Bay.
Stand fast admiring stranger, lest the gale blow you away.

If a word can epitomise the Terrace, it must be "grand".
For grand the Terrace is and grandiose is its stand.
Then blessings be on its might, with laud sincerely meant,
Sung loud, sung proud, sung gladly—sung grandiloquent.

A Prout's Bus outside the Lawns Hotel on the Terrace

The Garage Centre, Trelawney on the right and Central on the left

5

Transport at its Best

The world awaits all who step on a Prout's bus!
Foreign parts beckon! No hindrance, no fuss!
In livery green sparkling bright in the sun,
John Roseveare, chauffeur, stamps the ticket to fun.

Mark, solid at helm, is a management dream,
Tall, dark and handsome, a boy of Brylcreem.
Brother John meek and mild, yet taut as a wire,
Driving's his alter ego—they call him "Hellfire".

In transport legendary, these masters of road,
Conduct you in style, grace and favour bestowed.
Plush seats to relax every passenger's mien.
They know where to go, so you'll know where you've been.

To Tintagel, Boscastle, Wadebridge and Polzeath.
Barnstaple, Bideford and yes, even St Teath.
There's Truro there's Lanson, Tavistock and Dartmoor,
Looe , Polperro, Land's End—such great treats in store!

Plymouth for the panto, for shopping and teas,
Prout's buses cross over the Tamar with ease.
None better, none safer, no one can disparage,
These heroes emergent from Trelawney garage!

6

At the Pictures

Every Friday night we go to cinema at the Rivoli.
And most of the films make us laugh, but some we regard more trivially
For the penchant of boys who gather up in front on a sixpenny bench—
Hard seat, but harder yet when what is on the screen makes our buttocks clench.

The Rivoli, magnificently galvanised, is owned by Charlie Lobb.
A man of the people is Charlie, allegedly worth a fair few bob.
His father-in-law, Old Rosie, is the usher on the floor.
His sister-in-law, Miss Roseveare, issues tickets at the door.

Mr Oliver, who comes from St Teath, is the technical wizard.
He comes down to the Rivoli each Friday, undeterred by gale or blizzard.
Bringing along films in big round cans, and associated twin projectors.
The inevitable lapses in synchronicity are grist for the mill of objectors.

And oh, what absolute delights there are to be seen
On the vertically hanging white sheet euphemistically named the silver screen.
Fred and Ginger, Bud and Lou, and the three (or is it four?) brothers Marx.
Tarzan, Jane and Boy; Great Expectations, O what larks!

The Church Rooms at the foot of New Road. A corner of the Rivoli can be seen on the right

Cops and robbers, cowboys, Indians, a gripping weekly serial;
A big film and sometimes a little film, some solid, others ethereal.
A full supporting programme in which the good guys always win.
Three Musketeers, bold pirates, Robin Hood with Errol Flynn.

With images in black and white, film noir and even duller,
Relief comes swift, and worth the wait, in glorious Technicolour.
And when 'tis done, we stand for the King, and head for home right civilly.
Next week we know we shall return to the ever-blessed Rivoli.

7

The Church Rooms

The Church Rooms—how many are they?
An internal pair at last count.
A big hall for social engagements,
Plus an ante-room—two the amount.

What really goes on when they're open?
For open they are, now and then.
Can you get in if you're from the chapel?
If you can, will you get out again?

All are welcome for special occasions—
Jumble sales and Remembrance Day;
August fête (worse than death), boxing contest;
Talent concert, and maybe a play.

Public meetings to quiz parish council,
Local art exhibition, whist drive;
Harvest festival auction (with Rosie);
On these one (or both) Church Rooms thrive.

Evacuee school during wartime,
The ante-room also involved—
Though its not very big when you're in it.
But with tea urn removed, problem solved.

Best of all, Christmas Sunday School party,
And prize giving (church only this one).
The most joyous of festive occasions.
Who'd have thought that the church was such fun?

The Church Rooms is a most barn-like building,
In appearance quite passably rural.
St Peter's undoubtedly owns it,
But why is its name in the plural?

Lobber Point, looking towards Port Isaac

The eastern side of the Awn with Hillson's Dump on the far right centre

8

Hillson's Dump

When it isn't any good,
Be it metal, be it wood,
And its usefulness is undemonstrative.
Be it soft or be it hard,
Be it painted, bare or tarred,
We take it and we heave it off the cliff.

Not just anywhere of course,
For to limit use of force,
A special place is kindly designated.
By the path to Hillson's house,
Out of sight to man and mouse,
For Port Isaac public's use it was created.

At the top of old Fore Street
By Cliff Cottage place your feet,
Making sure that Lobber Point is full in view,
Walk the path for twenty yards,
Then if right you've played your cards,
You are there—now dump whatever pleases you.

The cliff drops sheer and pure
To the surging sea and shore,
With the rear of eastern breakwater beside.
A worn chute at the top
To direct the mighty drop,
And the rubbish disappears on the ebb tide.

To enshrine its well-earned fame
We give disposal a nickname,
And "Hillson's Dump" is just that sobriquet.
Be it flexible or stiff
We just heave it off the cliff,
Then we turn around and slowly steal away.

The breakwaters as seen from Hillson's Dump

The breakwaters at low tide

Middle Street

9

The Breakwaters

These mighty altars in the harbour lane,
One under Lobber, feeding from the west.
One from the east, beneath Cliff Cottage pressed.
Their blunt ends strive, yet never meet the twain.

Raw concrete hath fulfilled their sainted role,
To claim grand heights of fortitude unfettered.
Worthy of pride with words in bright flame lettered.
Intrepid bastions of the harbour's soul.

From out the ebb, as behemoths they rise,
Lank weed draped fine on limpet studded walls
Emergent ladders as the ocean falls.
Leviathans at rest 'neath calming skies.

The little boats ride in on flood tide wave,
Cheered by the open arms at harbour mouth.
Safe haven! Set the course due south!
Eternal Father, ever strong to save.

Pawlyn's Cellars

10

Pawlyn's Cellars

Pawlyn's Cellars you'll find right downtown.
They're under the aegis of Mr Tom Brown.
'Skarrock Hill on the left, the Lake on the right,
Sign over the entrance, a welcoming sight.

Flight of steps on the outside lead up to an office,
Precinct of harbourmaster Anthony Provis.
Panorama of harbour, beach and Town Platt,
Gulls, a dead dogfish, quite often a rat.

The Pawlyn's are brothers who hail from afar,
(Some place or another familiar with tar).
Buyers for fishes brought into the Port,
They purchase and ship just about all that's caught.

The doors onto Fore Street are weathered and quaint.
The hinges want oil and the wood could use paint.
As inwards they swing with a merciless squeal,
A world of twilight to the gaze they reveal.

Outside of the doors and set into the wall,
A barometer true records each rise and fall.
For years beyond count fishing fleet it has served,
The weather predicted was not undeserved.

The floor of coarse concrete, abraded with age,
Diligently hosed down, rankness to assuage.
Fish scales and expectorant an odd mixture make,
From floor to the drain, and then out to the Lake.

Dim inner room where hallowed colloquy,
Brings debate uninformed and ripe soliloquy.
Stacked withy piles to be woven in pots,
Tales of fair wind and catches, of ships and of yachts.

Pawlyn's is in place for commercial reasons,
It hustles and bustles throughout all four seasons.
The fish come and go, infinite in variety,
Habitués revelling in half-felt sobriety.

To think! In this tattered caravanserai,
No jug of wine brightens the most humdrum day.
Book of verse doomed to lie unopened, unread,
And yet is there thou, with new-loaf Sherratt's bread.

11

Trewetha Lane

Trewetha Lane is two miles long.
It twists and winds—it flows
From Mine Pit Corner as a song,
To where the main road goes.

A lovely way it is to stroll
At all times of the year.
The hedgerows bloom, the soft clouds roll,
Sweet primroses appear.

Though leaves may fall and twigs may point
In leaden winter hue,
The Lane will never disappoint
The traveller ambling through.

Set foot on welcoming ascent,
The Doctor's house at right.
Old Vicarage next—stay and repent!
The coalman's store in sight.

Let George's steps and Margaret's Lane
Not hold you in their thrall.
The level road will ease your strain—
Behold the Temperance Hall!

Valencia House trumpets renown,
Carlenice view commands.
Rose Hill comes up from full downtown,
Where First and Last now stands.

A glimpse of valley and Church Hill,
Then cellars crowd around.
There Harry Sweet and Jess and Will
Steer, fish on sacred ground.

The Lane climbs through bank-creeper load
To Council housing rows,
Gaunt dwellings, windy Hartland Road,
Aligned with flapping clothes.

Onwards! The Lane has far to go,
Lundy Road, Tintagel Head.
Prefabs, an ultra-modern show,
Where once did cattle tread.

Fear not! The cattle yet remain
On Hillson's pasture lands,
In farmyard secret, blunt and plain,
Milked daily by his hands.

Port Gaverne valley is displayed,
Treore on distant brake.
A rise, a curve, and there arrayed,
The farm of brothers Blake.

Trewetha hamlet, ever chaste,
Policeman's house on right,
All hollyhocks and stays tight-laced,
Archer Farm just out of sight.

A coppiced hump, all that remains
Of Wheal Boys, once proud mine
For antimony, stress and strains
That noble men define.

And then Bodannon, with its barn,
Sunk roof and bowing walls,
The Lane in steady course moves on,
Colstanton's legend calls.

For here a mighty curve swift swings,
Round Frogpool, greening weed,
From whence Port Isaac valley springs,
Beloved Lake to feed.

Midnight! The Cheyney Hunt rides there.
Ghost hooves hard on the field.
See it and perish! Thus beware!
Haste traveller, do not yield!

There is but a mere half mile more
To end Trewetha Lane.
Pol'worgey Farm, let steps be sure
The mighty hill to gain.

Pol'worgey Hill, the last ascent,
Minepit Corner but a boast.
The top is reached with no relent,
There's Cornwall's southern coast!

Brown Willy, Roughtor, china clay
Works, white St Austell sett.
Treharrock woods, Tresungers gray,
Endellion's silhouette.

Trewetha Lane! Now all is done.
Full wondrous from the start.
Glorious the B three-three-four-one,
As slowly we depart.

St Peter's Church at the junction of Back Hill with Trewetha Lane

Inside St Peter's Church

12

The Chairs in St Peter's Church

What have they seen, these everlasting chairs,
Brown patina, in steady rows arranged?
Do they dispel the congregation's cares?
Are they devout, from sinfulness estranged?

Could they but speak, these time worn artefacts,
There silent set in age respected ranks,
They might describe the scent of candle wax,
Recalling blessings, goodly praise and thanks.

Behold them line by line in silent prayer.
A century of service they have known.
Though generations pass, still they are there.
Inseparable bond, St Peter's own.

Their joints are weak, yet stand their dowels proud.
The scourge of woodworm take they in full style.
Their feet are weary, yet with backs unbowed,
In columns firm they line the ample aisle.

Above their heads such mellow words have flown
From sermons countless over pulpit's rim.
Te Deum, Nunc Dimittis they have known.
Each has from *A & M* a favourite hymn.

Their seats have borne a legion of the just,
For many were they who chose where to sit.
Through fashion's change they kept their sacred trust.
On shelves they held their share of holy writ.

The glorious host of those who loved these chairs,
Now rest forever 'neath Endellion's sod.
They were our best, our noblest, our forebears.
They sing with angels and they walk with God.

The School as seen from the allotments

The upper beach Fore Street profile from the school to the Pentice wall

13

Games in the School Playground

What games that playground knew and loved!
The cliff scant feet away just o'er the wall.
A Squashems line against a buttress shoved,
And out-around the surge of mass football.

In cloakroom dark a Rough House oft held sway.
At side of Lifeboat House leaned Weasel sticks.
The skipping ropes, loose knickers blue and grey.
At back of Little Hill Podge took its kicks.

A line of rigid backs for Rusty Bum,
Collapsing two, four, six, eight and ten ton.
Full in-around beat Cockarusha's drum,
And fights enthralled the playtime mob's mid-run.

We hid and sought, yet found no place to hide,
Save o'er the wall in blackthorn thicket, sheer
Above Long Pool and quickly rising tide,
We coursed like rabbits till the coast was clear.

Marbles and alleys clicked along the flat.
Conkers were swung with metronomic glee.
Cheese Cutters sliced the gristle from the fat—
King over one, or two, or perchance three.

The peace of in-around was ruptured oft.
The straits were held to be non-sacrosanct.
The big boys barrier defied the soft.
For little ones in droves may God be thanked.

One quarter of an hour was all there was
To raise the mayhem in the savage beast.
Two times a day, yet time enough till Boss
Did ring the bell to damp the happy feast.

14

A Flea Hunt

When on my head I feel an itch,
I scratch it at my peril.
My mother's eyes latch on and twitch,
As if my hair was feral.

She grabs at my offending hand
And hauls me to the table,
Where I must sit—procedure planned—
As fast as I am able.

In front of me she spreads a sheet
Of last Sunday's "Dispatch".
"Come on Steve" isn't there to greet;
His purpose is to catch.

Not catch my glance—my head's pushed low,
So close he isn't there.
On him will drop, perhaps fast, perhaps slow,
Whatever's in my hair.

Thus stoically I take the blame
And let my senses roam.
I know the next rule of the game
Brings out the fine toothed comb.

My hair quite reasonably unkempt,
Since that's my normal angle,
Its cleanliness less real than dreamt,
The comb finds every tangle.

It pulls them here, it pulls them there,
Each stroke brings tugging pain.
Just when it seems my scalp must tear,
The comb comes back again.

My mother revels in the fray,
Her aim is victory.
The comb's her weapon all the way,
Her quarry is a flea.

An itchy head, a simple scratch—
Immediate connection
To flea (or fleas); she is their match,
Relentless her inspection.

And if on newsprint white and black
A flea's induced to fall,
With fingernail she makes it crack,
To end its cranial crawl.

So you this progress can avoid,
Don't scratch when Mum can see.
Let fine toothed comb rest unemployed,
And save the worthy flea.

15

Doctor

The surgery's appended to his dwelling,
As if it were a vital afterthought
To great ideas, full rich beyond the telling,
Deep principled, by healing mentor taught.

His house palatial stands upon a bluff,
Round weathered near the foot of dear Back Hill.
A tamarisk surround where breezes sough.
Trewetha Lane starts there—for good or ill.

A place of solace this, to ease the load.
The pump awaiting call at time of drought.
St Peter's church inviting o'er the road.
Come ye who travail, free your minds from doubt.

The surgery contains two rooms discreet,
An outer where all would-be patients wait
Their turn to see the doctor, who they meet
In inner sanctum room, abode of fate.

A fire set for the waiting, flick'ring bright,
To offer cheer to all who feel its need.
The mantel groans 'neath bottles, precious sight,
Prescribed in faith, the inner soul to feed.

The labelled physic eagerly is sought,
Accustomed hands receive their potions true,
Though colours vary, there is gladsome thought,
"The worse it tastes, the better it does you!"

The doctor's room, sober, professional.
Brusque diagnosis marks his lengthy art.
Behind a desk, virtual confessional,
Exuding competence he sits, that mighty heart.

Peerless is he in practice general,
Respect implicit in his course direction,
For treatment vegetable, animal or mineral,
Minor or major, ailment and infection.

He suffers fools not gladly, honest Scot.
His word is law, integrity his suit.
The halt and lame are cherished, fakers not,
Anathema to him are matters moot.

A generation of Port Isaac's native born,
His legacy are they, and e'er shall be.
He guides their steps through life—the old, the worn,
At journey's end he leads them peacefully.

More solid than a rock, wise as an owl,
What is his name, this well-beloved proctor?
In formal terms, Donald McDougall Sproull,
But his admiring flock know him as "Doctor".

Rough Seas at Castle Rock

16

The Policeman

His pace is grandly slow,
Deliberately so.
The uniform we see,
Defines authority.

He strolls each village street,
Intent upon his beat.
His presence typified
By dignity and pride.

His touch both firm and fair,
Those who offend beware.
Boys know from far and near
His clip about the ear.

A friend he is to all
Who on his service call.
His purpose to protect.
A man whom all respect.

Mr Pearce his name.
Widespread is his fame.
Praise him to the full!
Port Isaac's constable.

17

Fight!

Playtime!
Fifteen precious Minutes!
Make the buggers last,
And fill them up
With amiable chaos
Until the bell calls
Time!

And yet…….
Not all is sweetness,
Nor light.
Score settling counts,
And in playtime,
Windows of opportunity
Matter.

Fight!
Fight! Fight!
The call resounds!
The blood is stirring
And up to scratch
Step the adversaries
For pugilistic confrontation.
One may be willing,
One not.
But most of the time
Both aren't.

Fight!
And at the call
A ring four-deep
Surrounds the would-be battlers.
Perhaps fists swing,
Perhaps fists don't.
It doesn't matter,
As they always miss.

"Come on!"
Invites one.
"No you come on!"
Declaims the other.
"No, you come on!"
Reluctance reigns.
Until
At blessed ring of bell,
Playtime ends.
Each then is saved
To fight another day.

But more likely
The two shake hands,
Salvage honour,
And forget what it was all about.

Castle Rock, the Main and Tintagel Head

Hartland Road

18

Living in Council Houses

As neighbour unto neighbour moans,
Their ire gradually rouses.
They don't demur, they can throw stones,
They live in council houses.

Some old, some new, some in-between,
Blunt rows, defying gales.
On height of land, no trees to screen
The walls from wind's travails.

Right garrulous the residents,
Together, not by choice,
Invective without precedents
In full stentorian voice.

Few secrets here—the curtains jerk
As from behind she peers.
A favoured spot in which to lurk
And exercise her ears.

Rough-cast the sides, as if to match
The characters within,
An epithet one could attach
Without the least chagrin.

Each house has an internal bath,
With taps that seldom leak.
Thus, not to trample hygiene's path,
It gets used once a week.

A washhouse too, with copper stout,
And mangle close to hand.
Such mod-cons are, without a doubt,
The finest in the land.

The coal is piled on floor of shed,
Just inside the back door,
Unless the bath is used instead—
It probably holds more.

The water's tanked up in the loft,
Kept out of sight and feeling.
But when Jack Frost's breath in does waft,
It pours down through the ceiling.

Along the eaves the winds do boom,
The windows creak and rattle.
The draft runs free in every room,
Assailing goods and chattel.

A fireplace cheers the wintry soul
With coal-inspired heat,
Which reaches out to warm the whole,
O'er radius of two feet.

Looking to Church Hill across Canadian Terrace

And when the rent man comes to call,
As quick as they are able,
The residents cry "One and all!"
And hide beneath the table.

The garden has a modest slope—
The weeds don't seem to mind,
Washing hangs sodden, without hope,
The chickens scratch behind.

A rat (or two) sometime comes by,
Out of the field beyond,
From Tom Saundry's noisome pigsty,
And fragrant slurry pond.

Yet lift the gaze, and there it lies,
Half of Port Isaac Bay,
With Delabole against the skies,
Trebarwith cross the way.

Tintagel Head both square and stark,
Behind it, Hartland Point,
And Lundy's lighthouse after dark
The horizon doth anoint.

Though they are poor, rich is their view,
They may wear ragged trousers,
Yet they are blessed through and through—
They live in council houses.

South of Lobber Point

19

Church Hill

From Slipway House it rises, innocent
The gaze of Pawlyn's Cellars at its feet.
Rapier-like its one-in-five ascent,
And at the summit, Kilroy's well-used seat.

Climb if you will this ankle-weary road,
Yet pause to rest at valley entry path.
By quarry recess ease your heavy load.
At Hancock's redoubt rub the aching calf.

The houses cluster first on the right hand,
Deep-terraced 'gainst the soaring, brambled height.
Below on slated rooftops grey gulls stand.
On valley floor burst apple blossoms bright.

The dwellings end at quarry's lower flank,
Where Jimmy Baker tilled potatoes prime.
The Killing House moulders on valley bank
Encroaching blackthorn tangle bides its time.

Brave and devout ascend this holy way—
Endellion bound, with loved ones to converse.
Past Homer Park, Trefreock, travel they,
Beneath the lark-loud sky all cares disperse.

Church Hill! Progress ye pilgrims as ye climb,
And falter not on solemn gradient.
With gladness tread the testing ruts sublime,
Descend the very way that up you went.

Bounds Cliff above St Illick's Well

St Illicks Well

20

St Illick's Well

Along the path twixt Tartar and Bounds Cliff
A little valley droops in modesty,
As if it were a secret, come upon
To lift the spirit on a cliff-edge jaunt,
And challenge with its rocky-stepped descent.
Its course is short—from source to where the sea
Pays homage to its mouth, would take no more
Than ten good minutes to enjoy on foot;
Into the brake, where lush green fills the bed
In marshy seep which starts incipient stream
Girt fine with rushes, reeds and iris spears.
Then, where the shady slopes commence to rise,
Banked marguerites display as drifts of stars,
With foxgloves rising, dappled-pink and proud,
Heads bowed as if for sanctity they wait.
On, where the bramble-edged path stumbles down,
To meet the stream at crossing of set stones,
The water flows from hollow dank beneath,
Born from the clay in soft heart of the vale,
Sequestered in a magic timelessness.
For here in faith, St Illick's found his well,
And centuries have marvelled at its power.
Holy and pure, it sends down to the sea,
To meet dark slate smoothed dapper by the waves,
A stream known gladly to the peregrine
Whose eyrie rests on Tartar's crumbling heights.
Atop the downstream slopes sea pinks clump strong,
One on another, like a range of hills

Tiny, thrift-decked and circumspect.
And here and there a robust bush of heath
Casts purple glow in amethystine drops.
The best is at the very end, for there
The stream drops free over a lip of slate,
To fall in majesty a score of feet,
And falling, breaks into a glistening veil,
A bridal fall, each droplet sparkling bright
As west'ring sun drops down to Varley Head.

On Little Hill

21

On Little Hill

One bench abuts school wall,
The air is warm and still.
The gossips come to call,
For this is Little Hill.

One bench backs on Fore Street,
The harbour deep before.
Sit down and rest your feet,
And garner local lore.

You can dark rumours spread
And reputations pillage.
For here no good is said
Of people in this village.

How joyous is this place!
How widespread its renown!
Come, show your second face,
And do your neighbour down.

A good note could be heard
In manner of a token.
This, chiefly when a word
On newly dead is spoken.

The living slake their ire,
For benefit or ill,
Parleying base desire,
Gathered on Little Hill.

22

The Old Mines

Nature has risen and claimed them for her own—
Where once bold miners hacked at ore and stone
The waste piles slumber, under rank weed grown,
And deep down, drips chink in the dark, alone.

In moss-spread ruins the memories resonate,
Blind shafts, abandoned both to time and fate,
Black adits peer from cliffs of glowering slate,
That men of hope made haste to penetrate.

Wheal Boys—Trewetha Mine—the shining light
From whence emerged wheel ore, Endellionite,
The world of mineral science to delight.
Though centuries take their toll, its torch flames bright.

Roscarrock, Crowser, Pine Awn, Foxhole Rocks,
Dull gleam of jamesonite to line the box
Which waits with splintered rim for Tartar's blocks,
Fruit of bal-maidens taps and questing knocks.

Wheal Thomas, Rose, Pendoggett and Treore,
Bodannon, Poltreworgey's stope-set lore,
Rough winze in which, towards the earth's rich core,
The brave did venture down in search of ore.

Some shafts remain, half fenced and full forlorn,
Capped by soft elder and the rank blackthorn.
In fearful depths are mysteries to mourn,
And glories stern resolve chose to adorn.

In overt guise, great quarries pock the ways,
Tagg's Pit, Welshman's, Church Hill and Roy May's,
The lichen spreads, bench crispness sinks in haze,
And on the greening floors brown rabbits graze.

Amidst the wreckage, badgers nightly prowl,
On rotting timbers nests a tawny owl,
An errant fox emits a half-sensed growl,
The mine rests passive in its shroud and cowl.

A song of grace, hard-won antimony,
Abandoned works, long worn by wind and sea,
Last vestige of once vibrant industry
Adrift in mists of fading memory.

23

A Shilling on the Ground

His breeding was impeccable,
His voice full modulated.
We boys were coarse, execrable,
Our roughness underrated.

His arms jerked in a random way,
He flapped and dragged his feet,
Ungainly he walked out each day,
To reach his favourite seat.

The seat adjacent to Moon's Grave,
Half way down Gaverne Hill,
A view of sea, in wind and wave,
In sun and storm, or still.

He saw it not—behold his eyes,
His head on neck inclined.
His gaze directed at the skies,
His face to heaven resigned.

He tottered in his corpulence,
We followed in his wake,
We mocked his studied innocence,
Our jests we made him take.

We called out as we clustered round,
Although he paid no heed,
"There is a shilling on the ground!"
Soft dignity his creed.

I saw him at the seat one day,
A book lay at his side—
It was "These lovers fled away",
I crept downhill, and cried.

To once more meet him on the road,
And speak again his name,
I'd plead my guilt for taunt and goad,
And hang my head in shame.

Where he has gone, I wish him well.
I trust his head is crowned,
But let him find, in heaven or hell,
A shilling on the ground.

Port Isaac—the Temperance Hall bulks at left centre and the tower of St Endellion church is prominent in the far right distance

Upper Port Isaac and Tintagel Head in the distance

24

The Temperance Hall

The Temperance Hall
Is not very small.
Although, if the truly temperate
Were the only ones allowed to enter it,
Size would present no limit,
As there wouldn't be anyone in it.

The Temperance Hall
Is now for one and all.
The dear old Band of Hope
Has long since run itself out of time and rope,
And its banner—pride of its age—
Now gently surrenders to moths beneath the auditorium stage.

The Temperance Hall,
Never a shortfall.
Long may its doors remain
Open to the village populace in Lower Trewetha Lane.
They come to taste its glory
In matters musical and occasions repertory.

The Temperance Hall
Provides the wherewithal
For the audience on one side of the aisle to sing "Tipperary",
While those on the other side their rendition vary
By giving voice to "Pack up your troubles".
Then vice-versa, and so the cacophony redoubles.

The Temperance Hall,
Such a pleasure to recall.
An institution as well-loved as it is legendary,
Forever ranked first, never secondary.
It really is not very small,
But even if it was small it would still be bigger and better than
    nothing at all.

25

The Local Preacher

My drink is nominally pure water bright.
Stronger stuff serves medicinal reasons.
Since illness can strike me by day or by night,
Prevention rules all through the seasons.

My brandy resides in a dark cupboard's rear,
My sloe gin's on the top pantry shelf.
Ale I denounce in fierce sermons quite clear
To others, though not to myself.

Within "Golden Lion" shall not tread my feet.
As I pass my eyes look to the ground.
Yet when I'm a stranger in some unknown street,
To a pub I am sure to be bound.

I preach fire and brimstone, the perils of sin,
To my flock coming from near and far.
My mind is alive to their faults deep within,
And much narrower than Temple Bar.

My being exudes absolute sanctity
In neighbourly love full harmonious.
Yet for all I delight as I think this of me,
Others reckon I'm quite sanctimonious.

Dog collar I have not, vestments I eschew.
A suit with a tie does me well.
Saturday bringing bath night, with use of shampoo,
On Sunday I almost don't smell.

Local preacher I am, local man I remain,
Wesley and Roscarrock my beat.
I rally the chapel with words strong and plain,
Once, twice, then three times, and repeat.

I seek glory not, vainglory finds me,
Faith makes me as whole as it can.
Hope would be in my heart (if a place there was free),
Charity though, is not in my plan.

A view of the Town Platt from the perspective of Little Hill

On the Town Platt

Lower Fore Street showing the Pentice wall (left) the Post Office (middle right); Sherratt's shop (near right) and the Golden Lion pub

26

The Town Platt

"Platt" normally means "flat",
But the Town Platt isn't that.
And, (not to put it down),
Port Isaac's not a town.

Yet, Town Platt is the name,
And therein lies its fame,
A place where people meet,
Adjacent to Fore Street.

The Wheelhouse at the side
Once Tommy Atkins' pride.
The Slipway and the Lake,
The other side do take.

The lower boundary
At high tide meets the sea.
The harbour sits before,
Banked shingle on the shore.

Upon the Town Platt's slope
Lie punts, crab pots and rope.
With fishermen who talk
As to and fro they walk.

"Platt" normally means "flat",
And the Town Platt's far from that.
Misnomer it may be,
But its good enough for me.

27

The Post Office

At the outside quite unprepossessing
(Just down from the Pentice in fact),
With few frills and no window dressing,
And little of much to distract.

The shadow of the "Golden Lion",
Casts gloom on the portal austere.
An establishment all can rely on,
Serious business-like atmosphere.

It occupies base of triangle—
Fore Street does its frontage define.
Rose Hill on the left (not to wrangle),
On the right Shuggy's Ope's tight incline.

Jackie Hosking resides in that old Ope,
A seafarer, complete gentleman,
Calibre plated gold, faith and good hope,
Port Isaac's best, humour, élan.

The Post Office staff boasts Jinny Hills (Miss),
Who the needs of the populace meets,
Absolute probity her forte is,
Savings books, sorted mail, stamps in sheets.

Jinny's bearing verges on imperious,
Integrity writ on her large,
Only the brave and the serious
Are welcome when Jinny's in charge.

Bonhomie features not within her state,
Fools are not suffered gladly they know,
Luckily there is Olive (Mrs Bate),
At her side casting warm, kindly glow.

They work with united precision,
Discipline mandated on the floor,
Jinny never falls short on decision,
Dissenters are soon shown the door.

Matters postal could never be better.
Marked firmly with dedication—
Card, telegram, stamp and fond letter,
Olive, Jinny, reach out to the nation.

28

Sherratt's Bread

"Man shall not live by bread alone",
Quoth Jesus, Satan tempted.
Had He of Sherratt's bread but known,
His view would be pre-empted.

Five thousand fed He in a trice,
With five loaves and two fishes.
In Port Isaac a Sherratt's slice
Is all the body wishes.

A Sherratt's loaf—a half or whole—
John Newton said it best;
"'Tis manna to the hungry soul,
And to the weary, rest".

If bread was all that Sherratt's made,
It would not dim their star.
Magicians of the baker's trade,
None better, near or far.

They have much more—see saffron cake
Yeast buns and splitter batch
Arrayed upon the racks to take
With ultimate despatch.

And pasties are there by the score!
(They never go unsold).
All customers come back for more,
They love them, hot or cold.

The bakery! Family run.
George, father, taciturn.
His wife, hair done up in a bun
With energy to burn.

Son John acerbic, hard to please;
Son Tommy, gentle, slow.
Contrasting personalities
With hands deep in the dough.

This day give they our daily bread
Blessed with the perfect leaven.
On such honeydew are we fed,
A little touch of heaven.

A view of Lobber Cliff from a location outside the house of Westlake and Alice Brown on Rose Hill

Lobber field and Khandallah, looking over the roof of Canadian Terrace

29

First Line of Defence

Lobber isn't the front line of battle,
But it plays a key role in the war.
The defenders look not unlike cattle,
With the merest suggestion of gore.

The trenches lie deep at cliff edges,
Commanding the harbour's tight mouth.
Coils of rusty barbed wire stand on ledges,
All-direction deterrent — save south.

The Home Guard patrol when the tide's out,
Without hope, without fear, without gun.
The folk of the village have no doubt,
That, (perhaps), they will scare off the Hun.

Invaders of Port Isaac's harbour
Can no quarter, no mercy expect.
The vigilant guardians on Lobber
The village defend and protect.

For Lobber the high ground commanding,
Best bastion in Port Isaac Bay.
From Tintagel to Varley demanding
Sharp vigil by night and by day.

Should the enemy enter Port Gaverne,
Out of sight of the Lobber Field chaps,
He will find himself there no safe haven,
The beach is awash with tank traps.

The ramparts of Lobber enduring,
No foe can prevail 'gainst their might.
Port Isaac's well-being securing
Till blackouts devolve to lamplight.

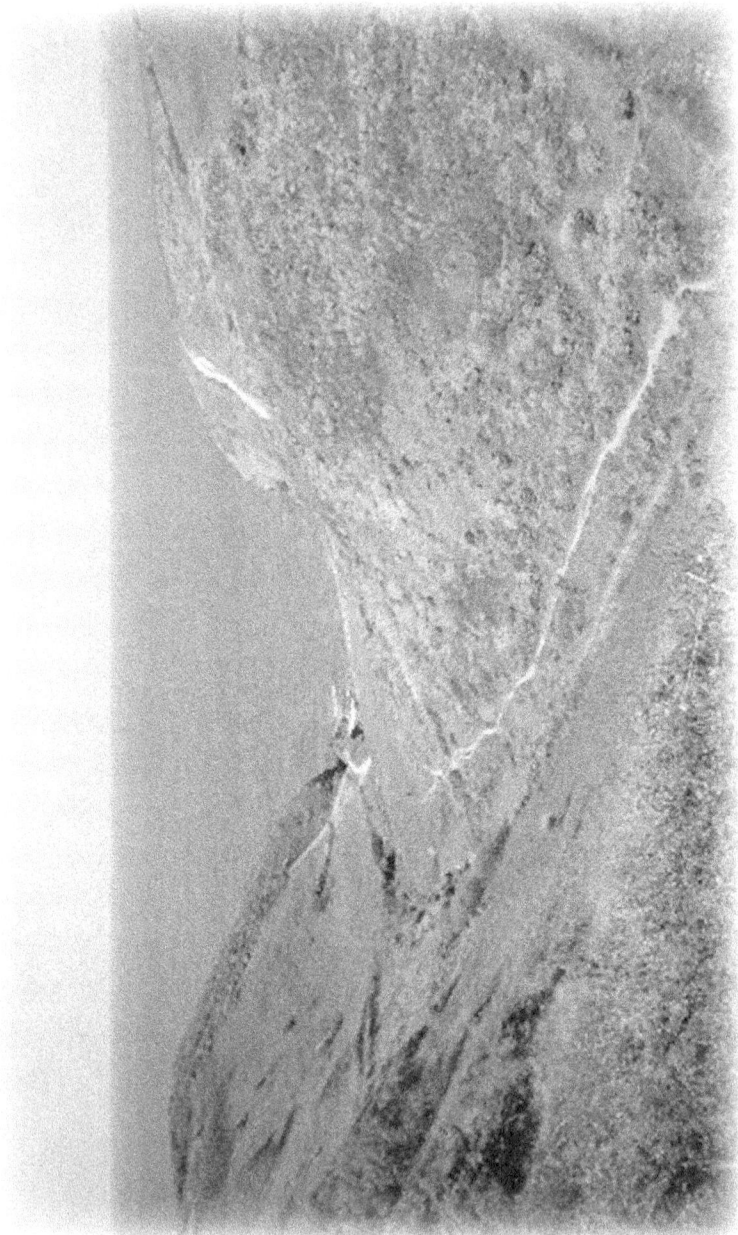

Freak Valley in the autumn, looking down to Pine Awn

West of Castle Rock

Freak valley in the springtime looking towards Trefreock

30

The Freak Valley

Trefreock hamlet; cottage, muddy lea,
Down rutted lane that ends against a wall.
A stile; a holy well; far glimpse of sea.
Rejuvenated vale and waterfall.

A valley; deep-cut stream drops steep and true;
An oakey standing proud; a water wheel
Now mute—a bluebell wood, a path runs through,
A shaded bridge, Roscarrock on the hill.

Some twisted willows, iris bright below,
Full yellow, sabred leaves, cow-dinted clay.
A bramble riot, scent of fox and crow,
And fronds of cress that in the eddies play.

A rising slope, old quarry high above,
Thorn choked, a frog pool silent in its maw.
Green sheeted weed on which no ripples move,
A magpie's nest, the chack of a jackdaw.

The Lobber track, some slippery stones to tread,
A kneeling place, sipped water from the stream,
Steep onward path to Crowser, Varley Head,
Shaped hollow, vestige of a miner's dream.

Primroses myriad by Midas pressed,
Soft springy turf along the flats beneath.
Full blooming gorse that hand of sun has blessed,
Green bracken, violets and purple heath.

The stream incised against a natural wall,
Rush screened and gurgling, to the ocean drawn.
The waiting beach, a tumbling waterfall.
The sky, the sea, the cliffs, the pools—Pine Awn.

A shingled reach, a scramble at the side,
A wave-cut shelf, sharp-faulted ridge and blocks,
Gullies and channels, flooded at high tide,
Black Annie vigilant upon the rocks.

Side view of St Endellion church

The tower at St Endellion church

31

St Endellion

A rusty gate set in a timeless wall,
Soft pennyworts and sweet primroses cling.
A path of worn slate flags from Delabole,
Blunt granite tower whence joyous bells do ring.

The portal calls, enduring wooden door,
Marked grey by weather, sanctified by time,
Bolt-studded, latch of hand-worn iron pure,
Daylight without—within, the light sublime.

Up in the portal's eaves, a swallow's nest,
Half-cup of mud, with dainty feathers lined.
Beneath, some faded notices attest
To jumble sales and whist drives once in mind.

Atop the tower behind the battlement
God stands on sheeted lead and views the world.
Town, village, hamlet, simple settlement,
From coast to coast all human life unfurled.

The rectory behind, the caw of rooks,
Great black pines, gaping cones upon the drive.
Church yard with canted stones in weed-choked nooks.
The well-loved yews, the hedge where robins thrive.

Tombstones recount such precious history,
Some granite, some of marble, others slate.
They speak of death, hope, love and mystery,
These humble lives, a pantheon small, yet great.

Endellion! Our final place of rest.
We come, not willingly, but come we must.
The good and lesser good, the worst and best.
Port Isaac's dust, such dust, such golden dust.

32

Gaggy

One day, he joined the choir,
Yet wasn't quite the type
For tongues of heavenly fire
To mollify his tripe.

But oh! How he could sing!
Sweet tenor, lilting, gay.
He'd made the pub walls ring
When rend'ring "Galway Bay".

In cassock he looked rare.
With surplice, rather racy.
Luxuriant his hair,
A hint of Spencer Tracy.

His personality,
Brought to the choir stall cheer,
Exuding bonhomie,
O'er waft of fags and beer.

He eschewed piety,
And "holier than thou"
Went with sobriety
The way of his last vow.

Not one then to rely on,
But oh so clubbable.
The spirit of a lion,
A rogue—but lovable.

Devil-may-care his game
Within the vestry pit,
Boys gloried in the name
Of him who didn't give a shit.

His smile was made to charm,
His cheerfulness contagious.
He did no mortal harm,
He thrived on the outrageous.

I'm glad I was his friend.
He gave such lasting pleasure.
His reed no wind could bend,
Until life's final measure.

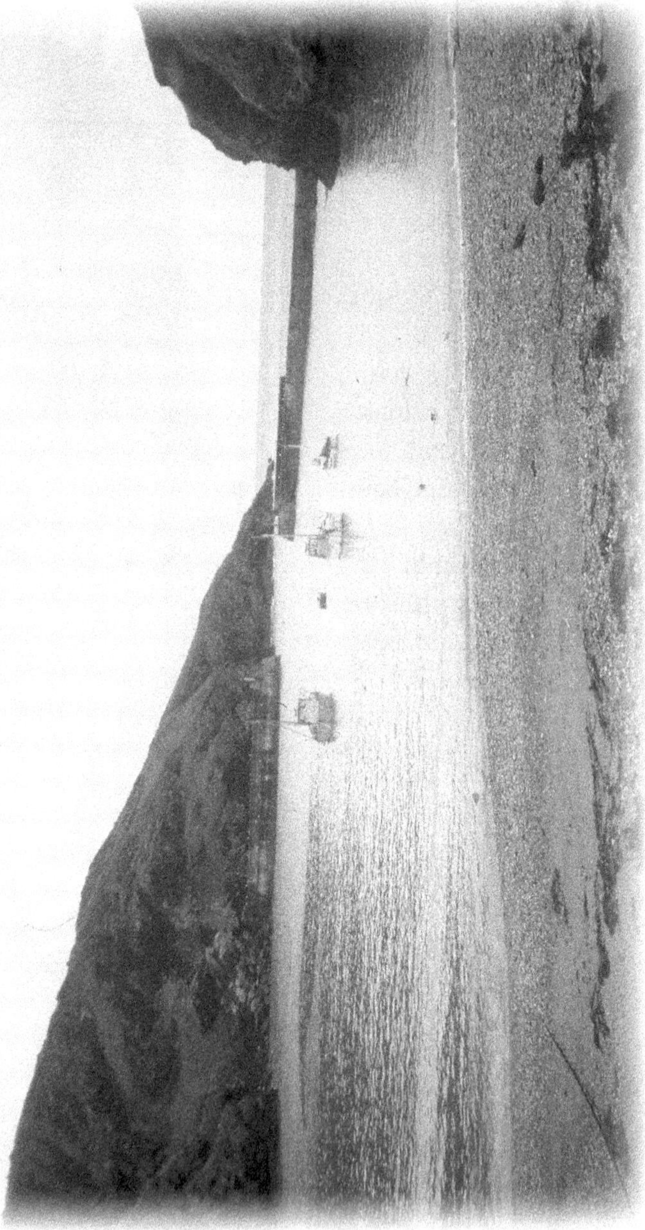

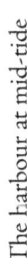

The harbour at mid-tide

33

A Callybash

A plank rough cut, sea-wormed and worn,
Of storm-tossed wreck found at Pine Awn.
One inch thick, six wide—in length
Four feet, enough to give it strength.

An orange crate, purloined one day
(When Old Tair Bunt had looked away),
Nailed to the plank back at the rear,
To form a seat from which to steer.

A pram dumped up in 'Wetha brake.
The body stays, the wheels we take.
No matter that the tyres are poor,
The spokes are sound, the axles sure.

One pair of wheels, secure of state,
Is nailed to plank 'neath orange crate.
The other, with a board to flank,
Is bolted loose to front of plank.

That done, to make the montage whole,
Some binder twine provides control
As reins to steer, preventing crash
Of downhill trundling callybash.

34

The Rolls Canardly

The hundredweights of coal are sacked,
And on the flat-backed lorry stacked.
No sides or tailgate intervene
To mar this hessian-decked scene.

Clad safely in protective leather,
Harold serves, come wind, come weather.
A crank or two, a sharp backfire,
A check on rim of tread-poor tyre.

The engine shudders, coughs, then rattles—
A veteran of many battles
With testing incline, rising hill.
And summer rain, and winter chill.

The lorry plays a starring role
Delivering domestic coal
To coal house, bunker, shed at back,
A blend of lumps, slate and wet slack.

Sedate of pace, its round it wends,
A means to manage noble ends.
To roam the village is its goal,
Wherever customers crave coal.

It creaks, it grinds in memory
Of better days that used to be.
Yet still it plies its regal course,
This venerable old workhorse.

Time leaves its maker's mark obscure,
Beneath a film of rich ordure.
Yet, since needs must, its name is hardly
More, or less, than Rolls Canardly.

It rolls downhill, consummate ease,
But labours up as on its knees.
Although it strives with might and main,
It 'ardly can get back again.

To benefit from motion slow,
The boys home in to get a tow.
They grab the rear and trot behind—
To Harold, out of sight and mind.

Coal and coke and anthracite,
Ensure Port Isaac's fires burn bright.
As evenings draw in, fireside cheer
Brings comfort to the waning year.

Tho' straining motor shows its age,
And clunks whenever gears engage,
Upon its service all rely,
Its heart is sure, its outlook Spry.

35

The Cobbler

Harry is his name.
Boot mending is his game.
He is a local preacher.
His wife is a school teacher.

He is not very big,
But we don't care a fig.
Good natured and so kind,
No better man you'll find.

He cobbles on demand,
Hobnails fly from his hand.
When you've just one pair of shoes,
There is no time to lose.

His shop is on Church Hill,
In ope both dark and still.
He crouches o'er his last
From dawn till dusk is past.

He works by touch and feel,
Replacing sole and heel.
He's never known to fail
To leave protruding nail.

Sea boots he'll vulcanise
Before your very eyes.
Protection from the weather,
With rubber or with leather.

If anyone aspires
To cut soles from car tyres,
There's no need to be shy,
Old Harry will comply.

At chapel Sunday school,
His one unfailing rule—
A Bible text impart
For boys to learn by heart.

They try to do their best,
But when put to the test,
Invited to recite,
They rarely get it right.

And yet no point in fearing,
Harry is hard of hearing.
Forgetting words they've read,
They say "rhubarb" instead.

To know him is a pleasure,
He is a local treasure.
A part of God's great plan,
A lovely gentle man.

36

The Mill Pool

There in the valley's deep and secret heart
Where meet two swiftly brown and gurgling streams,
The waters pool, and lo, no more apart,
Encircling dam makes surface mirror dreams.

The path diverges round the silent pond,
Deep-trodden hard by generation's feet.
To left, Trewetha bound and points beyond,
The right on to Pennant, Endellion and Plain Street.

Above the Mill these pent-up waters wait.
A slated gate in front seals off the race—
A channel shaped by turbulence and spate,
To wake the slum'bring wheel's hydraulic grace.

The Mill has not ground corn these many years.
Wheel's drive is rusted and its slats are furred
By creeping moss and drip of algal tears.
Its rumbling creak will nevermore be heard.

The mill race choked with mud and tangled weed,
Gone is the rush of water from its head.
And yet the mill pool thrives in time of need,
With fists of willow thrust from silted bed.

The fishermen, instinctive husbandry,
Coax wholesome withy harvest every year,
Cut neat to length both elegant and free,
And carried down to Pawlyn's from the mere.

The mill pool, first and foremost, valley's pride,
Home of the widgeon, frog and water hen.
Long may the dam keep vigil at its side,
Long may the waters rise and flow again.

Maria in Middle Street

The Lake Flush gate adjacent to Middle Street

37

The Lake Flush

Here comes old Ned, his flat cap at the rake.
His hobnails click and spark on Middle Street.
Black-clad and rheumy-eyed beside the Lake,
The steady lapping flush gate at his feet.

It spans the Lake on stoutly timbered frame,
Loose-pivoted to bounce on turbulence.
The boys, who are integral to the game,
Trail Ned, whose fortitude has drawn them hence.

Tom Saundry, from his shop tucked in behind,
Casts irate glare through window's long-lived smears.
The world to him may have been less than kind.
The flush defies him in his waning years.

Ned stoops to grasp the frame as he is urged.
He steps into the Lake with movements slow.
He lifts an iron bar which lay submerged,
He jams the flush gate shut and stems the flow.

Excitement trembles through the ranks of boys
As water aggregates on upstream side.
They wait with bated breath till, joy of joys!
Old Ned elects to loose the risen tide.

With two-by-four the iron bar is struck.
It falls aside to rest again in peace.
The gate is free, the torrent runs amok,
A mighty wave-front creams in full release.

Tom can relax—he sees the boys as one
Race Middle Street along, to Slipway bound.
Their bid to beat the wave—how fast they run!
The Lake in secret churns beneath the ground.

The torrent that Old Ned did thus create,
Sweeps all before it in the fettered Lake.
Through tunnels, narrow ways, the raging spate
Lets cleanliness rejoice within its wake.

The boys arrive too late, brave also-ran.
The wave expends its force upon the beach.
Its cargo spreads in a deltaic fan.
The gulls descend in clouds, a share for each.

Soon all is done. The scavengers depart,
And o'er the shingled stream falls blessed hush.
The happy boys are victors in the heart.
They wait to challenge Old Ned's next Lake flush.

38

Family Favourites

How much I wish to again sit and savour it,
An ever-blessed Two-way Family Favourite.

Just to hear the tones of Jean Metcalfe, or,
Direct from BAOR, Cliff Michelmore.

The essential accompaniment to our Sunday dinner,
They were adored by saint, beloved by sinner.

We thrilled to the strains at the very start
Of orchestral strings "With a Song in My Heart".

It was always a very safe bet that e'er long
Would come over the air "The Jimmy Brown Song".

And just to be certain we were never bored,
They gave us Tennessee Ernie Ford.

"Shotgun Boogie" or "Sixteen Tons" to choose,
Unless it was "Milk 'em in the morning blues".

"Where the blue of the night meets the gold of the day",
Bing Crosby invariably led the way.

"Cocktails for two", sound and static flickers
With the help of Spike Jones and his City Slickers.

"La Mer" rolled in with Charles Trenet.
"Que sera, sera" sang Doris Day.

Vaughn Monroe chased "Ghost Riders in the Sky".
"Cool Clear Water" for all, except Dan and I.

"Shifting Whispering Sands" were then arrayed,
We were "In the Mood" for "Moonlight Serenade".

"Sparky's Magic Piano" will come on — won't it?
Unless that is, "Life Get's Tedious, don't it?"

"The Laughing Policeman" and "Runaway Train".
Gene Kelly at his best, "Singin' in the Rain".

"When Father Papered the Parlour", that was fun.
"My Grandfather's Clock" — fated no more to run.

"Never Trust a Woman" was advised by Phil Harris,
Who the "Darktown Poker Club" did financially embarrass.

When Vera Lynn rendered "The White Cliffs of Dover",
The Two-Way exchange was practically over.

But she let us know also "We'll meet again".
Feet tramping to Anne Shelton's "Lily Marlene".

And perhaps one last gem before it was through,
Kate Smith's superb version "I'll be seeing you".

Without the joy of each Two-way Family Favourite,
Sunday dinner would have had much less to flavour it.

"With a song in my heart" it was time to go,
Alas to endure Billy Cotton's Band Show.

Along the cliffs from Crowset, past Crowser Island, and on to Varley Sands and Varley Head

Varley Sands

39

Varley Sands

Port Isaac Bay knows many strands—
Trebarwith, Gaverne, Isaac, Quin, Pine Awn.
Yet none so fine as gem-like Varley Sands,
Clear water, golden beach, by master drawn.

No tropic shore can with its charm compare,
Twixt Crowser Island and bold Varley Head.
The cliffs fall sheer around this hollow fair.
Only the tide has all its secrets read.

The dappled boulders in the water shift
As weed waves slow in secret eddy's hand.
With touch of breeze, the cat's paws gently drift.
Cloud's subtle shadow moves o'er rippled sand.

Only the brave gain access to its reach,
A scramble down the Head when tide is low,
To edge the slippery rocks and touch the beach,
First footprints dint on virgin sand below.

40

Writing Poetry for the Parish Magazine

Within the vestry sanctum, vicar
Sits and ponders. Candles flicker.

He fidgets, squirms; a squeak of wicker.
A glass, he thinks, of golden liquor?

It might just make his pen flow quicker,
And sheets of verse stack ever thicker.

Without, cassocked choristers bicker.
Church wardens o'er collection dicker.

Gaggy, his surrogate ass-kicker,
Emits, as usual, knowing snicker.

He stills his musing, out of time
To find THAT word to make a rhyme.

His title's the perennial sticker—
How to devise a rhyme for vicar?

If he could shorten it to "vic",
His fancy would his conscience prick.

And yet—if of him there were two,
A wondrous couplet could ensue.

To think! How well a pair of vicars
Would follow up a pair of knickers.

Doyden Point and Castle and the entry to Port Quin harbour

West of Castle Rock 157

Port Quin

41

Port Quin

Behind encroaching ivy lie
Sad ruins. Home to peace and joy
In former days when there did hie
Good wife and daughter, man and boy.

A cottage row stood there, once home
To fishermen of stout Port Quin.
The roofs are caved, the oven cloam,
All broken shards, is strewn within.

Wormed wooden lintels lose their way
On empty windows, gaping doors.
And crumbling walls with feet of clay,
Shed mortar on the rotting floors.

A fireplace hollow, dank, long cold,
Stick-choked through jackdaw diligence.
The chimney breast greens slick with mould.
Light drops as tears through blackthorn dense.

Who were the folk who called this home?
Did joy divert their daily toil?
Where have they gone? Where do they roam?
These families sprung from Port Quin's soil?

Across the road a cast iron pump
On corner stands, in silence versed.
It rusts, yet when sound's Zion's trump,
May solace bring to some who thirst.

The damson trees crowd on the side,
Their growth is rampant, lichen clad.
A tangled aspect they provide,
Their heyday past, their prospects sad.

Lost Port Quin folk, yet does your blood
Course red in best North Cornish vein,
As did it once, when at the flood,
Your fleet braved dark and stormy main.

To legend then they slipped from sight.
Return to port for them denied.
Their cottages consumed by night.
In harbour, all that moves is tide.

42

The Singing Butchers

Their industry surpasses that of weavers,
As rationed joints surrender to their cleavers.
How surgical their skill—their art is long.
Caveat emptor, lest they render song.

Close harmony from father and from son,
Young Jack, united voice with old Boss John.
No subterfuge, no guile, no game or tricks,
Established Family Butchers, J. N. Hicks.

John is often gruff, Jack sometimes cranky.
Their silver lining shines through cloud of Sankey.
A chapel hymn will make them seem quite skittish.
John seeks the honest touch, "Madam, be British!"

Trapped customers as captives do they greet,
On the sacrificial road to Sunday's meat.
They rise in song at least encouragement.
Time inches by, the clock ticks pure dissent.

Shall we at the river gather, must we wonder?
How soon till promised roll is called up yonder?
If we could only gain that sweet by-and-by,
Few of us would not be h-a-p-p-y.

If the food of love is music, we may tarry awhile.
If not, we'll grit our teeth and force a smile.
For whether or not the ambiance is far too much sirs,
Escape is not an option from the singing butchers.

43

Skittery Grass

By Maria Platt-Cornoldi

Skittery Grass, what a funny book!
Skittery Grass was our game.
Port Isaac was the playing ground
Where as boys we had so much fun.
Port Isaac was our playing ground.

Oh, skittery, kittery grass!
Oh what fun that was!
Sliding down those slopes.
Whooping and shouting as we skittered down.
Port Isaac was our playing ground.

Skittery Grass—what a funny book you are.
Hey Eyesnot, where is anon?
Oh Texas, get Rodge, Buh, Mo.
Where are Shadow, Joey and Syd?
And oh, don't forget young Ted.
Port Isaac was our playing ground.

Skittery, kittery grass.

Ernest at Long Pool with the Eastern breakwater wall in the background.

Long Pool looking up towards the Town Platt

44

The Long Pool

Compared to all the many other pools
Left by the ebb in worn declivities,
By harbour's edge where rock's might ever rules,
Long Pool stands alone, in regal sensitivities.

And long it is—the longest pool we have,
Looking at the sky in mirrored solitude,
Until the flood, with steady surge of wave
Reclaims it for its own deep rectitude.

Its bottom smoothed right even by man's hand,
A seaweed carpet, green and olive brown.
Held in its waters, robust store pots stand,
Great withy monarchs, submerged to the crown.

Pot ballast formed by sea-worn blocks of slate,
Secured by binder twine tight-bound and tarred,
The entry ports are closed by metal plate,
The captive contents zealously to guard.

For there do cumulate most crustaceans
Caught by the fishermen out along the Bay,
Fated they are, for seafood-hungry nations,
To dishes grace in restaurants gourmet.

The commerce rests with Pawlyn's lusty traders,
These crabs and lobsters with disabled claws,
Nicked by fisher-folk in thigh-high waders,
Who tread Long Pool, custodians of laws.

The little gug, just out of Long Pool's reach,
Cuts underneath the school, perched high above,
Where pupils sit and daydream of the beach,
And golden moments o'er the rocks to rove.

Where they will fish for moles, bent pin and thread,
Or seek out bishops in the cool-touch weed,
And tin boats float, the keels defined by lead,
And cork flotillas launch, from bondage freed.

Long Pool draws fond respect from every age.
We come and go, but Long Pool e'er shall be,
A sacred jewel in Isaac's heritage,
Its waters clear, its spirit bright and free.

Downtown Port Isaac with Church Hill on the right and Top Shed in the valley beyond

Lower Dolphin Street with the corner of the Bark House in the left foreground

45

The Bark House

The day has come! For Barking Day is here!
No other place than Dolphin Street will do.
The doors are opened onto ruddy cheer
As fire delights the copper's tannic brew.

The Bark House! Neighbouring the House Trevan,
Where Frederick the physician plied his trade.
And up above lurks Temple Bar's tight span,
And over there the Dolphin ales purveyed.

The stage is set! Each player takes his place,
The nets all folded, ready for the pot.
The boys thrill with a sense approaching grace,
The shim'ring grate is central to the plot.

As one by one the nets in copper steep,
Infused, inspired, protected 'gainst the sea.
The boys towards the glowing hearth do creep,
Scarce able to contain their mounting glee.

They clutch potatoes tight in willing hands,
Purloined from home while mother looked away,
To cast in coals, according to their plans
When the announcement came for Barking Day.

They watch the tubers yielding to the heat,
To char and split beneath the furnace draw.
Then patience gone, imperative to eat,
They rake them out, no matter if still raw.

Too hot to hold, they toss into the air
The smoking tetties, till they start to cool.
Their teeth soon strip the skin with expert flair,
A trick they learned from dinner time at school.

Tho' semi-baked, unseason'd, flecked in coal,
The taste is heaven to ragged-ass gourmets.
Food for the boys, the gods, the mortal soul.
The Bark House! Let its name resound in praise!

46

Gulls' Eggs

The carapace is olive-brown,
Dark blotches cluster at the crown,
Some dark, some muted; random spots
And streaks and squiggles, dabs and blots.

Yet now and then a shade of blue
The shell imbues—then spots are few.
A prize for a collecting boy,
A find to fill his heart with joy.

The season's first is what we seek.
Thus well before May's premier week
We scour the cliffs and give our best,
Heedless of risk to reach each nest.

In hollow scooped upon a ledge,
Three eggs to lay, three chicks to fledge,
With seaweed shreds and dry grass lined,
The nest is perfectly defined.

We take some eggs for reasons two,
Collection first, contents blown through.
And then, so appetite's not foiled,
The others are served up hard boiled.

Some say gulls' eggs go well in cake,
(For boys a little hard to take).
For we prefer them chopped and spread
On a new thick slice of Sherratt's bread.

The fishermen, avoiding shoals,
Do sometimes land on rocky Mouls
To fill their mawns without a care,
With gulls' eggs in which we all share.

As May moves on a glut arrives,
Eggs to outnumber bees in hives.
Next year, tho' fate may do its worst,
We're out again to hunt the first.

Fore Street and the good old Public lavatory alongside Little Hill with the steps to Ted's Harbour cottage residence alongside Chapmans shop at the left foreground

47

My Friend Ted

As Michelangelo was to stone,
As Tyrannosaurus was to bone,
As Primo Carnera was to height,
As Bela Lugosi was to fright,
As Ancient Britain was to trees,
As Ben Gunn, marooned, was to cheese,
As Miss Hoare's garden was to flowers,
As Babel's profile was to towers,
As Edgar Wallace was to books,
As Marguerite Patten was to cooks,
As John Profumo was to fibs,
As Adam was to useful ribs,
As Tommy Handley was to laughs,
As Tommy Woodruffe was to gaffes,
As Oscar Wilde was to fine wit,
So was old Ted to pure bullshit.

48

The Likes of They

Their class is upper, ours is lower.
They speak fast, while we speak slower.
Though "R" is "arr", they say it "ah",
We have to walk, they use a cah.

We know our place, we know they think
The stool they void comes without stink.
These saloon bar, gin-sipping folk,
Regard our customs as a joke.

And yet sometimes we hide a grin,
We're locals true, they're runners-in.
The place they live must be quite nice,
In place of house, they own a hice.

When over dinner we are hunching,
They sit to dine, and consume luncheon.
We drink strong tea, they imbibe coffee,
They look at us o'er nose of toffee.

And if we see them on the street,
We touch our forelocks should we meet.
We step aside, they seize the way,
And hardly pass the time of day.

They know that they were born to rule,
That was all learned at public school.
Hence all in all its not surprising
Their attitude's so patronising.

Pray tell, in which benighted tavern
Did they decide that Gaverne's Gavverne?
Our aspirations they decry,
Our opportunities they deny.

O, just to meet and talk to one!
And tell him, friend, your day is done!
I wish you health and good luck! Toff,
Do us a favour, please fu clear off!

Maria with the Port Gaverne Valley and Treore in the background

Temple Bar

49

Temple Bar

You won't get a car
Through Temple Bar,
Unless you're a boy
With a Dinky toy.

From side to side
Its not very wide,
And its modest height,
Makes it pretty tight.

From Fore Street, sally
Along an alley,
Through Temple Bar,
And there you are—

In Dolphin Street,
Where the elite
The cottages fill
Up and down the hill.

With all that said,
When they crave bread,
They can only stop
At Sherratt's shop.

No if or but,
The one short cut
Is to follow the star
Through Temple Bar.

Yet only the thin
Can dare go in.
Anyone stout
Will not get out.

For bread in hand,
Plump Granny Chadband
Must direct her feet
Down to Middle Street.

Then to the Platt
That's nearly that
She uses her merits
To ascend to Sherratt's.

It doesn't defeat her,
She completes the detour,
But she wouldn't get far
Through Temple Bar.

50

Scrumpers

Apples hang on the bough!
The time to pluck is now!
The moment seized today—
The farmer's far away.

We negotiate the fence,
Barbed wire my jacket rents.
We scurry round and pick,
We're in and out right quick.

Though pockets we do stuff,
There's never space enough!
We shove more up our jumpers,
For we are scrumpers!

51

Rose Hill

From First and Last
Rose Hill falls fast.

First walk, then run
By Dick Hampton.

Bull terrier bold
Makes blood run cold.

Then Cowboy Joe,
Tall, stout and slow.

Once Lord of Mill,
In valley still.

Valencia glowers
O'er Miss Hoare's flowers.

On terraced beds
They nod their heads.

Nearby to see,
John Neal's fig tree.

To climb upon
Once John is gone.

By Oaten's tarry,
Andy and Harry.

With sister Sue
And Bill Pink too.

A timely sally
Down Back Alley.

Or set the feet
On Dolphin Street.

Chicago House
The heart will rouse.

At least three stories,
Architectural glories.

All men must hark
To Townsend, Mark.

Handsome, lanky,
They call him Yankee.

A short step down
Lives Westlake Brown.

With Sister Alice
In White House palace.

Off to the right
A pleasing sight.

The Bird Cage plain
On Margaret's Lane.

Cottage of Lobb,
A proper job.

Beside Mount Pleasant
Both past and present.

And Shuggy's Ope,
Tight as a rope.

Sam Honey below,
Not far to go.

At Rose Hill's feet
Is good Fore Street.

The Pentice wall,
First port of call.

52

Community Values

Our community is close knit,
And it doesn't take a half-wit
(Although we have enough of those around),
To know, come wind, come weather
What holds us all together,
Secure upon Port Isaac's hallowed ground.

Our village life is tribal,
Which means we're often liable
To despise all other places in this role.
We don't much like Tintagel,
But opprobrium is gradual,
We reserve our best abuse for Delabole.

There's no chance to avoid a
Dash of schadenfreude
In any of our dealings with each other.
A highlight of our labours
Is to denigrate our neighbours,
(And the same applies to sister and to brother).

Linked like horse to carriage,
We are skilled in inter-marriage,
And we count extended families in dozens.
There's no doubt that its all leading
To intuitive inbreeding,
So that most of those we dislike are our cousins.

God holds us in his hand, hence
We keep his ten commandments,
Or, if we should tell the truth, p'raps eight or nine.
Alright then, almost seven,
That's enough to get to heaven.
Well then, five or six — at least most of the time.

It could be three or four,
It depends on what they're for —
Such as keeping to the Sabbath's holy day.
When we hear "Thou shalt not",
We give it all we've got,
And we do our best to walk the other way.

We love a family feud
From the mists of ages brewed,
We can keep it going strong for generations.
To set the fires alight
Mere perception of a slight
Is all we need as cause for celebrations.

Eschewing generosity
Of spirit, our pomposity
Of purpose is what keeps us firm on track.
We aim to help our neighbours
In return for bigger favours,
And we hold them to it till they pay us back.

Our legendary cunning
Ought to set the many running,
They'll regret it if they fall into our clutch.

We cloak our guile in wit
(Tho' we're really full of shit),
And a conscience never bothers us too much.

'Tis said we're passing mean.
Who cares! Its our demesne!
If we had money we might all be misers.
The early worm's advance
Just doesn't stand a chance,
Port Isaac is renowned for early risers.

Taking avarice and sloth,
We'll settle please for both,
Plus any of the other deadly five.
At envy we excel,
Vainglory serves us well,
Getting angry makes us glad to be alive.

For lust we have no use
(A fair enough excuse),
Adultery we'd try out if we could.
But although it would be grand, it
Is too hard to understand it.
We'd be gluttons if we only had the food.

Some try to rise above it,
Yet we were born to covet
What others have and what we wish was ours.
It doesn't do to hate them,
But we do love to berate them,
And can keep it up for many happy hours.

If we were Musketeers,
We'd clip each other's ears,
And "one for all" turn into "one for one".
And regarding all the rest,
There's never a contest,
In a populace which dotes on "all for none".

Yet the motto of Cornwall
Calls out to "One <u>and</u> All"—
We don't like it, but we choose to let it pass.
We never lose our touch,
The "All" don't count for much,
Unless its when we kick them up the ass.

With absolute propriety,
Port Isaac's Great Society
Rejoices in its strong communal glue.
Mutual dislike unites us,
Doing neighbours down delights us,
And that's good old Port Isaac through and through.

53

Remember the Sabbath Day

The Sabbath is a rest day,
The trouble is, I can't play.
Remember to keep it holy.
The routine grinds by slowly.

At nine I rise from bed,
A bowl of milk and bread,
For breakfast I partake,
With tea for Mum to make.

The ornaments of brass
Are polished in one pass,
With Brasso in Dad's hand.
They on the mantel stand.

Black lead goes on the grate,
Make haste, or I'll be late,
To polish oven door
Is a pre-Matins chore.

With ashes raked out whole,
Newspaper, kindling, coal—
Sequentially arrayed,
The fire is neatly laid.

Now Mum prepares the joint,
Brown gravy to anoint.
Ah Bisto! What delight!
Potatoes peeled last night.

The turnip in a pot,
And parsnips piping hot.
Don't like them? Hopes are dashed.
With turnip they are mashed.

And now I have to run
To church—life is no fun.
Don cassock, surplice, ruff,
Brush hair, that's near enough.

I serve up at the altar,
With the vicar and his psalter.
Snuff candles, get collection,
Try not to lose direction.

Matins hour feels overlong.
(It's the same for Evensong).
I hope its not a crime,
To dream of dinnertime.

The service ends at last!
To home I hurry fast.
The plates are on the table.
I'm ready, willing, able.

Dad slices up the meat,
As we prepare to eat.
The vegetables are done.
We eat up every one.

The wireless is switched on
Once all the food is gone,
(The part, that is, for Sunday),
The rest we eat on Monday.

"Two-Way Family Favourites",
Cheerful and also graver bits.
Jean and Cliff Michelmore
Do all requests ensure.

"With a song in my heart",
Its time for me to start
And sip the bitter gruel,
I'm off to Sunday school.

Ripe men, cast from the pub,
Go home to wolf their grub.
A shout (or two) and slaps,
On sofas they collapse.

As I run to the church,
On Back Hill some do lurch.
Tobacco, sweat and beer,
The aura in their rear.

At Sunday school I share
In hymn, in psalm, and prayer.
Miss Tyler's homilies,
They bring me to my knees.

And when this hour is done,
There's still no chance for fun.
The valleys, cliffs and beach,
On Sundays banned from reach.

I am allowed to talk,
And go for a "nice walk"
Along Trewetha Lane,
Or on Port Gaverne Main.

My knees must show no blood,
My shoes be free of mud.
With the Sabbath in the way,
Bird's eggs are safe today.

The time has come for tea,
I head home happily.
Great treat for eyes and belly,
Blancmange and cake and jelly.

With luck, some ice cream too,
A block, tri-coloured through,
Whole or perhaps a half, we
Buy it from Cliffside café.

One final church-wrought thing,
St Peter's bell doth ring.
Oft times I go along
To serve at Evensong.

Magnificat, Nunc Dimittis,
Sermon over, thank God it is.
Now St Chrysostom's prayer,
Blessing, then open air!

Gulls on the Pentice roof

I dash down to see Gran
And Granfer—in roasting pan
Is saved some dinner's meat
And tetties for me to eat.

From there with my best friend
To Little Hill we wend,
At Gents to make a call,
And writing read on wall.

Sunday brings bath night,
Before the fireside bright.
Tidemarks fade like setting sun,
Darkness, day's course run.

54

Happy Days

Such faint applause!
The actors pause,
Port Isaac's stage derided.
Cornish heart
Might play a part,
Had one not been denied it.

Celebrity jostles
In costly hostels,
Councils house great unwashed.
Blare and grin,
Doctors of spin,
Opportunities get quashed.

Chapel feet
Drag in retreat,
Church is much the same.
Institutions slip
From authorities grip,
Royalty is lame.

Scottish schism,
Nationalism,
North Ireland weeping cancer.
Welsh assembly
Like pitch at Wembley,
Westminster devoid of answer.

State of manners
Waves no banners,
Village out of sorts.
The people groaning,
Always moaning,
Second rate at sports.

The Cornish reel
'Neath laws of steel,
While justice flakes like rust.
Magistrates foolish,
Policemen ghoulish,
Politicians forfeit trust.

Education thrice
Throws losing dice,
Health service a curse.
Buses and trains
Chant sad refrains,
Affordable housing worse.

A sorry story
Decline of glory
For saint as well as sinner.
Yet in the Port
We can set it at nought
When a pasty's there for dinner!

East of Varley Head

55

Journey's End

I chose to ramble east of Varley Head,
There on Pine Awn's soft turf I laid my head
And chased the paths of dreams where e'er they led.

My guiding muse the way did then appoint.
Soft dew-decked daisies did my feet anoint
And let them lead me south of Lobber Point.

Encouraged thus I strode, for good or ill,
Through memories dear, just north of Little Hill.
So many gone! I see their faces still.

The barque has sailed, sad, empty is the dock.
Would that I could but still the ticking clock,
And rest forever, west of Castle Rock.

Afterword

"We lives by rules made somewhere else by sons a bitches don't know nothin' about this place".

Annie Proulx ("The Shipping News")

www.ingramcontent.com/pod-product-compliance
Lightning Source LLC
Chambersburg PA
CBHW022356040426
42450CB00005B/209